In case of loss, please return to:

_____

_____

_____

_____

As a reward: $ _____

# GET UNCOMFORTABLE

SERVE THE POOR. STOP INJUSTICE. CHANGE THE WORLD... IN JESUS' NAME.

Published by LifeWay Press®
© 2007 Todd Phillips

ISBN: 1-4158-5299-5
Item Number: 005035540

Dewey Decimal Classification Number: 261.83
Subject Heading: MINISTRY \ POVERTY \ CHURCH AND SOCIAL
PROBLEMS \ JUSTICE

Printed in the United States of America

Leadership and Adult Publishing
LifeWay Church Resources
One LifeWay Plaza
Nashville, Tennessee 37234-0175

We believe the Bible has God for its author; salvation for its end; and
truth, without any mixture of error, for its matter and that all Scripture is
totally true and trustworthy. The 2000 statement of The Baptist Faith and
Message is our doctrinal guideline.

# TABLE OF CONTENTS

SERVE THE POOR. STOP INJUSTICE. CHANGE THE WORLD... IN JESUS' NAME.

## MEET THE AUTHOR
# TODD PHILLIPS

**I'm Todd Phillips** . . . Christ-follower, husband, and dad. I love movies, books, wrestling with my three kids, recounting each day with my wife in the evening, and mountaineering. Right now, my family and I live in Sterling, Virginia, near Washington, D.C. I am the pastor of Frontline, a generational church-within-a-church at McLean Bible Church near Washington, D.C., where more than 3,000 young adults worship each week on four campuses. My primary passion is reaching "pre-Christians" with the life saving message of Jesus Christ.

Before I got to Frontline, I served as the communicator for three generationally-targeted ministries in Texas: Austin Metro, San Antonio Metro, and The Soul Cafe in Kerrville. During that time, I also wrote *Spiritual CPR: Reviving a Flat-lined Generation*. I earned a Master of Divinity at Southwestern Baptist Theological Seminary and am currently working on my Doctorate of Ministry at Princeton Theological Seminary.

Thanks for being willing to *Get Uncomfortable*. For the first twelve years that I followed Christ, I completely missed the link between evangelism and service. The paradigm shift that resulted in my life led to profound changes in me, in the congregation of young adults I serve, and ultimately led to this Bible study. I hope what follows can do the same for you.

Come by and visit me at *www.toddphillips.net*.

# LETTING GO OF THE TABLE

When my son Parker was learning how to walk, he would use the coffee table in our living room to pull himself up and then walk around the table for hours at a time. He spent days walking around and around that table, smiling and giggling the whole time. For a time, he was very content not to venture beyond the safety of the table. After about a week, he seemed to be getting a little bored (or dizzy) from the monotony of walking in circles, but he didn't know what to do next.

Then, for no obvious reason, one morning he walked to the corner of the table, but instead of turning to follow the table around the corner, he took an extra step forward and found himself standing on his own, hands in the air. I could tell he was thinking, "Wow! Here I am out here in the middle of the room with no table holding me up!" He began to giggle and then fell right down on his bottom. That was the beginning. From that moment on, he never walked around that table again. He would go to that same corner, pull himself up, turn away from the table, and take a step. Everything had changed.

## NEVER GOING BACK

The moment a child takes his or her first steps is special but not strictly because of the steps. If the journey ended at that point, then the whole process would be woefully anti-climactic. Letting go of the table is thrilling because of what it symbolizes; for when a child lets go, they are never going back. Those first, tentative, uncertain steps mean that the proverbial gun has been shot at the beginning of a great race.

This same child who found out several years ago that he could stand on his own two feet is now running around the soccer field like Pelé. He is amazing! He runs with purpose. He no longer has to devote all of his attention to each tentative step. He doesn't have to think, "I now need to put my right foot forward to keep from falling." There's no longer any forethought in the process; his body simply moves. It runs. It's agile. Running is no longer something that Parker tries to do; running is now part of who Parker is.

The baby steps were a good and necessary part of the process of making Parker a runner. The goal however was not tentative steps in the living room but intuitive movement in the world. The goal is to be a runner—to make running second nature in order to open up the world beyond the coffee table.

In the very same way, each of us will have an opportunity through this study to let go of the table. Many of us are living our Christian lives holding on to the programs, events, and comfort of our local church. Many of us have never ventured out from these programs—Sunday service, Wednesday dinner, weekly Bible study, and the annual Christmas gift drive. When no one is around, we wonder, "Is this all there is?" "Is this all that we're supposed to do and be as the people of God?" "Is there something more to this Christian life?" "Did God put us on this earth just to keep the believers happy in their church buildings?" All of these church activities are good and have their place in the process, but they are just that—a part of a much larger process.

## ZECHARIAH 7:9–10A
THE LORD OF HOSTS SAYS THIS: "RENDER TRUE JUSTICE. SHOW FAITHFUL LOVE AND COMPASSION TO ONE ANOTHER. DO NOT OPPRESS THE WIDOW OR THE FATHERLESS, THE STRANGER OR THE POOR . . ."

### EMBRACING SELF-FORGETFULNESS

In the Christian life, the programs of the local congregation that are centered on meeting the needs of the members are the Christian equivalent of walking around the coffee table. They were never meant to be the sum of the Christian life. A mature believer develops what I call a "healthy sense of self-forgetfulness" rather than an unhealthy preoccupation with self. Jesus demanded that if we would truly follow him, then we must deny ourselves (Luke 9:23). There is an unbelievably huge world out there in need of believers who have denied themselves, let go of the table, and become runners in God's race to increase His eternal kingdom through Jesus Christ.

I'm not talking about more activities, because we certainly don't need that. We are all very busy Christians. But busy believers are not necessarily mature believers. Just because we are going to a lot of activities doesn't mean we are growing in our faith. Just because we're engaged in daily devotion doesn't mean we are becoming a fully devoted follower of Christ. We all must move from internally focused involvement in the church to externally focused engagement with our world in the name of Christ. We must all, at some moment in time, let go of the table.

## A MATURE BELIEVER DEVELOPS WHAT I CALL A "HEALTHY SENSE OF SELF-FORGETFULNESS" RATHER THAN AN UNHEALTHY PREOCCUPATION WITH SELF.

### BECOMING A PART OF THE SOLUTION

Through this study, we will each have an opportunity to do just that—let go—and venture out into the world on our own two feet into the realm of poverty and injustice. In doing so, we can embrace a largely neglected piece of the heart of God. We will come to see that God passionately desires to do something about suffering in the world. Further, we will come to understand that He has invited us to be a part of His solution.

Through our acts of giving and assistance, our spirit will become attuned to the giving nature of God Himself. Our spiritual muscles will start to flex at the opportunity to give. We will no longer sit back and think, "I wonder if I should," as though our involvement is optional. We will become Pavlovian in our response to need. This is where God wants His children—He wants us to be so attuned to the suffering and pain of those around us that we respond to those needs without thinking. Giving to the needs of others, personally involving ourselves in the hopelessness of others, and diving into the misery of others in the name of Christ will become our second nature.

I've seen it happen countless times. Once a believer begins to give and pour out—once a believer has let go of the table and realized that not only can we balance on our own two feet, but we can walk . . . and not only can we walk, but we can actually run—everything changes.

## WHAT ABOUT YOU?
## HAVE YOU HELD ONTO THE TABLE LONG ENOUGH?

# BEGINNING THE CONVERSATION

We have all come from very different backgrounds and very different life experiences. However, we have been brought by God to this moment in time with this book in our hands. God has a message for us regarding the way we live our lives. Get ready. We all have the opportunity to change in ways we can't yet imagine.

God's Word is far from silent in regard to these issues of social change. A tremendous amount of Scripture deals directly and specifically with the issues of poverty, injustice, and oppression. We're going to ask God some tough questions and get answers from Him in regard to our personal and corporate responsibility and opportunity to serve the poor, needy, widows, orphans, and aliens in Jesus' name. Be prepared. God will also ask tough questions of us. He will reveal areas of our heart that may be numb to the needs of those around us. He'll show each of us how He wants to involve us in His redemptive purposes for the world. But before we get there, let's just begin the conversation . . .

What should I bring before the Lord when I come to bow before God on high? Should I come before Him with burnt offerings, with year-old calves? Would the Lord be pleased with thousands of rams, or with ten thousand streams of oil? Should I give my firstborn for my transgression, the child of my body for my own sin? He has told you men what is good and what it is the Lord requires of you: Only to act justly, to love faithfulness, and to walk humbly with your God.

MICAH 6:6-8

# BEGINNING THE CONVERSATION

## A PROBLEM OF GEOGRAPHY

Americans live in a cocoon. This cocoon—made from the interwoven silks of economic, political, and ideological freedoms—effectively isolates us from connecting to (or fully understanding) the way in which the vast majority of people on this planet live. Here are some basic figures about life outside that cocoon: one third of the world—that's about 2 billion people, men, women and children—lives on less than $2 a day. That's $60 a month, $720 a year. Some of us spend that much on our cars each month (car payment, insurance, gas, etc.). That ought to be enough for us to realize there's a need.

Do you agree that the U. S. lives in a cocoon, disconnected from the way the majority of the world lives? *Yes, We are blessed beyond measure and take so much for granted.*

What societal elements or cultural perspectives do you believe contribute to this? *We are disconnected from the way the rest of the world lives. We see things on TV and they are not real to us. We also think our way of life is best and that American are more important than those around the world who are not as well off.*

*We do not weep with those who weep around the world. We only weep with ourselves.*

**READ ROMANS 12 (yes, the whole thing).**

Discuss or reflect upon Romans 12 focusing on how this chapter applies to our responsibility to meet the needs of the poor and oppressed around the world.

Our national economy and political freedoms are not the only things that separate us from understanding the way the majority of the world lives. We further separate ourselves as believers by refusing to educate ourselves on the more than 2000 verses in Scripture that clearly reveal the following perspectives: God's heart for the poor and oppressed, the true condition of our world, our responsibility and opportunity to spread the gospel by serving others in need, and the promise that God will empower His children to accomplish His goal of justice and mercy for all the world through his Son, Jesus Christ.

As Christ-followers in the United States, we tend to feed ravenously on every passage of Scripture that refers to the blessings we receive from God. While we gorge ourselves on those verses, we by and large give very little time to the many passages that speak of self-denial, service, sacrifice, suffering for the sake of the Gospel, and sharing in the misery of others.

As quick as I am to judge our actions as the people of God toward the poor and oppressed, (I put myself at the front of the line) I'm equally as quick to absolve most believers from blame for our collective inactivity. In fact, I'm surprised that we aren't even less aware than we currently are of the global crises that plague the majority of humankind. Given how sparingly Scripture regarding God's desire for our involvement in social action is preached, it is amazing that these issues are acknowledged at all. This is our first and greatest problem.

The cynical side of me thinks that social justice is not preached because people who are poor and oppressed can't do the two things that most preachers want everyone to do—attend their churches and give to their causes. Additionally, my own experience as a pastor helps me understand that these topics are not addressed from the pulpit because "service" and "sacrifice" in Jesus' name is difficult to teach in today's consumer-driven church culture.

In such a culture, the preacher is only as good as his last sermon. He is rated by the straw poll every week as people gather in the lobby to talk about their approval or disapproval of the day's message. In this environment, many preachers stay away from the controversial subjects out of concern for reprisal in the form of lower attendance.

Download the *Get Uncomfortable* playlist. Get the list from your group leader or at *www.threadsmedia. com/media*. Make it your "soundtrack" for this study.

Do you agree that our churches have become part of the entertainment culture of our world? *Many of them have. Did we like the _____? Or _____ the pastor _____ _____ _____ it should be how did God speak to _____ _____ You and the Spirit*

How do you see your church in light of this charge? *Our church is not performing or entertaining. It is preaching the gospel in a way _____ as _____ to reach the lost. We are doing a pretty good job*

Secondly, our churches aren't structured toward responding effectively to these global issues. Many churches in the U.S. today, especially the larger they get, become like country clubs rather than spiritual hospitals. Over time we become concerned about our needs more than the needs of others. We become so focused on our own personal or corporate growth and maturity in Christ that we miss out on countless opportunities to grow and mature through service and sacrifice.

Church slowly becomes all about us and little else. Reggie McNeal puts it this way: "[Church] members obviously have needs for pastoral care and spiritual growth. It is critical that these issues be addressed. However, I am raising the question of how many church activities for the already-saved are justified where there are people out there who have never been touched with Jesus' love? The answer is a whole lot less than we've got going on now." [1]

Finally, the Christian publishing industry produces next to no material on these subjects. I was challenged on this statement by a young man recently when he asked me, "How can you make such an over-arching statement about Christian publishing? What's your source for the assertions?"

I pulled out a couple of the most recent annual product catalogs that I get in the mail and said to the young man, "Come over here, and let's see what Christians are reading these days." The two catalogs we looked at happened to be from well known publishing houses. From a potpourri of just over 2000 books, these were the alarming results: 69 books were on the topics of evangelism and missions (about 3.4 percent), 18 books were dealing with the issues of generosity, compassion or charity (0.9 percent), and no books—none—dealing primarily with the topics of poverty, injustices, and the church's response. I could almost see the scales falling from the eyes of this young man as he asked, "What do we do about this?"

That's exactly the question I'm trying to answer, at least in part, with this study. These numbers show that many of us have turned the Bible into a self-help program rather than a life-long process of self-denial. If Christianity is really just a personal improvement program we would have to ignore what Jesus told His disciples: "If anyone wants to come with Me, he must deny himself, take up his cross, and follow Me. For whoever wants to save his life will lose it, but whoever loses his life because of Me will find it. What will it benefit a man if he gains the whole world yet loses his life? Or what will a man give in exchange for his life?" (Matthew 16:24-26)

Read each of the following passages and then write a one sentence summary after each summarizing the purpose of the passage:

JOHN 10:37
JOHN 13:17
JEREMIAH 22:16
JAMES 1:22
TITUS 1:16

So what do we do? We can sit idly by and hurl accusations at the preachers of our churches. We can judge the country-club mentality of some of our congregations. We can even blame the publishing industry for leading us in the direction of self-indulgence. What will come of that criticism? Nothing. The only option we have for profound change is to re-engage in the Word of God and then *do* what it says. We must take ownership of our faith. We must read, understand, and put into practice what our God truly wants from his children in relation to those who are in need.

Read James 1:22-25.

How does this passage describe a Christ-follower who knows what God expects but chooses not to respond? *It says that such people are deluded and not acquainted with the truth. This scripture emphasizes the need to be doers as well as hearers. If you just hear & do not act it doesn't benefit anyone else.*

## IT'S ONLY THE BEGINNING

Over the next several weeks one thing is true: we have the potential to learn more about ourselves and about God through this study than we might expect. Through that process, we will be forced to compare our passions, values, and priorities with the passions, values, and priorities of God—and some of us will be found wanting. Some of us will see our true motivations exposed. But if we purposefully engage with this study and prayerfully consider God's character, the condition of our world, and our responsibility as members of the body of Christ, we will reap the rewards of a deeper and more intimate relationship with our Lord and a clarity of purpose that we may have never experienced. We'll see the world through spiritual lenses and begin to respond not with empathy or with apathy but with compassion that leads to action.

I can be so certain that we will each be transformed by our time with this study because it happened to me. A few years ago, I was one of the pastors who failed to teach about God's heart for the poor from the pulpit. I was a believer who contributed to the state of our publishing culture by purchasing and devouring Christian self-help books. I had little to no contact with those in need, and I was perfectly fine with that. My passion was evangelism—sharing God's love through Jesus with all who hadn't yet heard the gospel. I truly believed that I had been called by God to preach the gospel while others were gifted to serve the needy. And so I lived uncritically within the American cocoon.

Then I met Drew. Drew is a dear friend and a member of the church where I am pastor. Through a providential meeting with him just less than two years ago, God began the process of permanently altering my perspective on the Bible, evangelism, and the mission of the church. I began to study the Scripture through the eyes of my new friend. Months later, I remember confessing to Drew, "How have I completed five years of seminary, preached hundreds of sermons over the past 10 years, and missed over 2000, verses relating to God's heart for the poor?"

As a result of God's transforming love and nurturing through His Word as well as friendships with godly, selfless men like Drew, my heart has been changed to be in line with God's heart for those on this planet that are in greatest need.

Some of you will have a similar paradigm shift in relation to God's word. You'll see Scripture you know well and think, "He must be paraphrasing these passages." But you'll find as you search your own Bible trying to verify (or discount) what I've quoted in this study, that I've paraphrased nothing. I've not altered a single word of the text. Every passage quoted comes directly from the Bible. Believe me—I was as surprised as you may be. I continue to be surprised, and pleasantly so, at the grand plan God has for the world.

### REDISCOVERING OUR CHRISTIAN HERITAGE

Most people don't put the study of history on their "things I like to do when I have some spare time" list. But for the purposes of gaining a better picture of all that we're going to learn, we must know what the church has done in the past. We must know the actions our Christian forefathers took before we were here.

The church was not always disconnected from the issues of poverty and injustice. History teaches us that many cultural changes were actually birthed in the church. Godly people like you and me saw a need in someone else's life, met it, and changed the fabric of the world around them. The abolition of slavery, prison reform, the establishment of hospitals and schools for the poor, women's rights, opposition to forced prostitution, the fight against child labor, and numerous other human rights and social justice issues can be largely credited to the faithful actions of passionate believers.

American historian Sydney Ahlstrom of Yale University explained that the great humanitarian movement of the 19th century was "incomprehensible" without the "collective conscious of evangelical America." The movement was built, he said, on "the Puritan's basic confidence that the world could be constrained and reformed in accordance with God's revealed will," and furthered by the revivalists' "demand for holiness [and their] calling for socially relevant Christian commitment as the proper sequel to conversion."[2] All these statements are true, and the church has, in fact, had an exemplary record in the past of being light in this dark world.

But the people of God have also been the catalyst for the Inquisition, defended slavery in the South from the pulpits of countless churches, and created the Ku Klux Klan. Each time such atrocities are committed, however, they can be patently dismissed as works done by those who have misused, misunderstood, or ignored the mandates of God. On the other hand, whenever even one believer chooses to "fear God and keep His commands" (Ecclesiastes 12:13) and does what is right in God's eyes, miraculous things happen. Many victories for the poor and suffering throughout history have been won through totally devoted Christ-followers.

In light of this cursory look at our activist heritage, the church's current silence and inactivity is a new phenomenon. This is particularly ironic because we have more information at our fingertips than at any other time in history, yet we struggle to take action on either a local or global scale.

Listen to "Our Place at the Table" before your group gets together to discuss this session. (Your group leader will send it to you via email.) See if you agree about Todd and Drew's assessment of the state of the church.

Watch "More Than Stats" when your group meets. Is it uncomfortable for you to begin to see the true state of the world? Are you beginning to feel the weight of personal responsibility?

What are your reactions to this cursory look at the heritage of the church? *We have a lot to answer for an healing to bring. We must step up and be God's hands & feet to the in...*

Do you agree that right now the church is generally silent and inactive on issues that were previously important to her? *No, I believe that the church has gone through periods of activity but it has not been the rule. Many who were preaching the social gospel did not evangelize as much as necessary.*

## A PRIMER ON THE ISSUES

Although I have put a tremendous amount of prayer and study into the development of this study, it is, at best, only a primer. This is only the start of a life long pursuit of God's purpose for your life in relation to His plan of salvation for the world through His Son. I doubt we can draw from this study a well-structured philosophy of ministry toward the needy and suffering of the world. I don't expect that.

What I do expect, is that after our time together you will have seen your personal responsibility as a child of God to respond to injustice in the world. I also expect the Lord to peak your interest and pierce your heart as He did mine so that this primer can be a launching pad for further exploration, learning, and action. My hope is that you take away from our time together with a deeper understanding of God's perspective on these important issues and that you have some idea how you may rightly apply what you've learned in your own church setting.

Many of you will go to a place you have not been. You will travel on roads that your feet have never touched. This foreign place that God wants to show you will, in time, become familiar, and eventually, you will call it home. In some ways, you will become like Paul who was on his way to Damascus when his life was changed by the "light of Christ." The scales fell from his eyes; a whole new world opened up to him. His perspective changed. Many of us have been living our Christian life with scales or faulty lenses covering our eyes that prevent us from seeing the world through the eyes of Jesus.

## LETTING GO

Think for a moment how ridiculous it would be for me to ask my son, Parker, now that he's a runner, if he would like to spend a few days walking around the coffee table. He'd think I was punishing him for something he did. There's no way Parker would trade a Saturday of soccer, tree-climbing, bike-riding, and street football for a day of walking slowly around the coffee table. He used to love it, but that was before he realized that the world was so big and running was so exhilarating.

When we see what God has already "prepared ahead of time" (Ephesians 2:10) in relation to the needs of people in our world; when we see how big the world really is and how exhilarating it is to let go of the table and serve God with faith-filled abandon, we will never be satisfied merely attending Sunday services, Wednesday church dinners, weekly Bible studies, and annual Christmas gift drives. These will all continue to be good and meaningful parts of our Christian lives, but they will no longer be ends unto themselves. They will instead be places of empowerment and preparation for the great opportunities that lay before us. We will come to see that God has brought us together for such a time as this to change the world for what might be the last time.

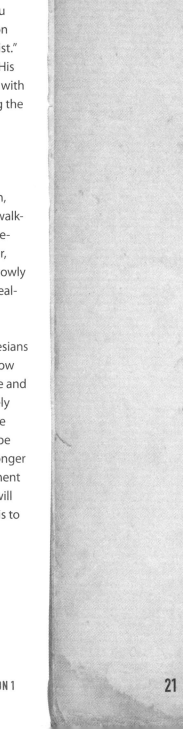

# PRAY

It has been said that prayer is not the preparation for the work; prayer is the work. That statement is a far cry from the reality of most of our experiences.

How many times have you been exhausted after praying rather than during it? How often have you been so burdened for others that you cannot fall to your knees quickly enough? Probably about as frequently as i have.

Let's not allow our past to dictate our future. We can look outside of ourselves and begin to earnestly petition God for the needs of others. That is the nature of intercessory prayer.

**Try this:** carry a small notebook in your pocket everywhere you go this week. Keep an eye and an ear out for potential prayer targets. Make a note of the homeless man on the street. Jot down some thoughts about the inner city school you drive past on the way home. Write down the names of people groups you hear about on the news.

At the end of each day, pray through your notes from that day. Pray for others before you pray for your own needs.

NAME: REBECCA SPENST

JOB OR MINISTRY: COMPASSION INTERNATIONAL CHILD SPONSOR

WWW.COMPASSION.COM

## IMPACTING THE LIFE OF A CHILD

Compassion International was something of a household name for Rebecca Spenst. Growing up in Colorado—the home of Compassion headquarters—and working in the Christian music industry meant that Rebecca continually heard about the organization's work. And while she "knew" a lot about Compassion, she had managed to miss the message—until she heard a firsthand story of their work.

"I was an event coordinator for a concert promoter, and a Compassion artist was performing at this particular event. Hearing the artist's account of traveling with Compassion to see the work Compassion does and how it has a direct impact on the children was all it took to persuade me to sponsor a child," she says. "Compassion is legitimate and trustworthy when it comes to sponsoring kids. That night I took a packet and sponsored a child."

Rebecca began sending her monthly check of $32 to Jeane, a young boy living in Haiti. Her sponsorship provided Jeane with basic needs and the luxury of school supplies. In the meantime, she sent letters and postcards. Every three to four months, Jeane sent a letter confirming that he was indeed using the school supplies, liked soccer, and especially liked school. "The thing I really enjoyed about sponsoring a child through Compassion was the correspondence," Rebecca says. "Jeane sent great letters, handwritten in his language, with translated versions on the other side. I've kept every letter."

Rebecca would still be sponsoring Jeane today if not for the fact that his family moved and there was no way to continue sponsorship with him. But the experience left her wanting to continue to invest in this way. "Compassion opened my eyes to the need for sponsorship and demonstrated the connection you can have with a child," Rebecca says. "I still feel connected to Jeane and know that I played a small part in his development."

Although she didn't pick up another Compassion child immediately, the opportunity to sponsor another child was just around the corner. Again, Rebecca finds herself mailing that monthly check.

"Some people discredit the value of sponsoring a child. It's not hands-on; you're not in that child's day-to-day life. But sponsoring a child has as big of an impact as anything you could do hands-on," Rebecca says. "There's a connection that's made between you and a sponsored child—they respond to you. They'll share their lives with you. You may never see this child face to face, and that's an act of service.

"Knowing that there's a child who's being cared for and provided for—that's the kind of thing that gives you purpose," she continues. "We're called to take care of widows and orphans. I am able to do that, almost mindlessly, while I'm going about my everyday life. Knowing that I'm making a difference in another country while I'm going about my life, working 9 to 5 feels good."

---

## WHAT DOES CHILD SPONSORSHIP INVOLVE?

When you sponsor a child through Compassion International, you are connected to one child with whom you have the opportunity to communicate. Your tax-deductible support connects your child with a church-based child sponsorship program that provides educational opportunities, health care and supplemental nutrition, safe recreation, and important life skills. It also allows your child to hear about Jesus and be encouraged to develop a lifelong relationship with Him. To learn more, visit www.compassion.com.

# THE CHARACTER OF GOD

Where do we start to examine issues as weighty as hunger, poverty, and injustice? Well, we don't start with the One Campaign or the Red Campaign or a Live Aid Concert. Instead, we start where everything begins in the Christian life: with God. God didn't look down from on high at the latest concert or campaign and say, "I guess that's what people are into these days." He didn't get the idea to care for the poor from our pop culture. God wasn't inspired to compassion for those in greatest need from anything outside of Himself. It all comes from within God. God *is* justice. God *is* compassion. God *is* morality. God *is* the protector of the poor and oppressed. These descriptive words are at the essence of who He is. God's love for the marginalized in society extends further and deeper than the passion of any rock star, politician, or preacher that is calling us to social action. We, then, need to study in depth the attributes of God that relate to His heart for the needy.

Jesus wept.
John 11:35

# THE CHARACTER OF GOD

## JUSTICE

Sometimes we try and use adjectives to describe what God is like. In doing that, we often forget that God is not "like" anything; other things are like God in some way or another. That is to say, God defines characteristics rather than being defined by things. Justice, then, is not some arbitrary system of right and wrong that we can use to evaluate the actions of God. Instead, justice, like so many other characteristics, is defined by God and His character.

But while we are quick to embrace certain attributes of God like love and grace, other of His characteristics frequently get pushed to the side. Among these is justice.

Define *justice* in your own words.

*— Taking care of widows & orphans Loving your neighbor The Golden Rule treating others the way you want to be treated.*

Define *injustice* in your own words.

*Profiting on others Exploiting others pain Not caring for others*

Read Colossians 3:12-17. Make a list the things that God calls us to do as believers. Now make a list of how God exemplifies those characteristics. Isn't it funny that God asks nothing of us that He does not fully embody Himself?

*Be kind forgiven believe in Christ Jesus Do not judge each other. Let go of pride arrogance*

Do you believe that justice is a forgotten attribute of God?

*Sometimes — We think the God of the Old and New Testament is different — but God is God & His heart never changes*

Gary Haugen, the president of International Justice Mission (IJM), says, "Justice has to do with the exercise of power. To say that God is a God of justice is to say that he is a God who cares about the right exercise of power and authority." . . . [3] "So, justice occurs on earth when power and authority between people is exercised in conformity to God's standards of moral excellence. So, we can conclude that *injustice* occurs when power is misused, violating God's laws, to take from others what God has given them, namely, their life, dignity, liberty, or the fruits of their love and labor." [4]

Haugen's definition of justice is founded in what God says about Himself. Throughout Scripture, God clearly expresses His passion for justice in the world as a whole as well as in those that follow Him:

" . . . the LORD is a just God. Happy are all who wait patiently for Him" (Isaiah 30:18b).

"For I the LORD love justice; I hate robbery and injustice" (Isaiah 61:8a).

"He has told you men what is good and what it is the LORD requires of you: Only to act justly, to love faithfulness, and to walk humbly with your God" (Micah 6:8).

Descriptions of God's justice continue past the Old Testament. Some of the most compelling pictures of His justice are visible in the life, actions, and words of Jesus Himself. Christ was born into a cultural system in which a few people held the majority of the power. If you happened to be outside of that specific group, then you often found yourself marginalized and excluded. In light of that cultural standard, it is particularly amazing to see the respect and decency Jesus granted to those who received none from their contemporaries. Most visible in the book of Luke, Jesus spent time on the fringes with women, tax collectors, the diseased, and the poor. Further, He taught about the proper distribution of wealth and the need of generosity.

Through Christ's life on earth we see that justice wasn't just a noble cause or philosophy by which He lived. He never saw justice as merely a good idea that His followers might want to consider if they wanted to be "better Christians." We see instead, through the words and deeds of Christ, that justice was not what Jesus did; justice is who Jesus was and continues to be. He was described as "a man of suffering who knew what sickness was" (Isaiah 53:3). Jesus shares in our sufferings as He did with Mary in John 11 where we read that "Jesus wept" (John 11:35).

Listen to "What Else?" before your group gets together to discuss this session. (Your group leader will send it to you via email.) Do you think there is a part of God's character that you have neglected?

We are to be "imitators" of Christ (1 Thessalonians 1:6). We can do so by understanding that justice is not simply something to support or a cause worth fighting for; justice should be one of the characteristics that defines us as people.

Read Matthew 21:33-46.

What "fruits of the kingdom" do you think Jesus wanted from the Pharisees?

*Love & Compassion, caring for others instead of enforcing man made laws. Humility & gentleness*

## COMPASSION

We see through Scripture that God is greatly pained by the misuse of power or position by any human being, but He is especially grieved when His children do so. His pain is real—not figurative or philosophical. He suffers with those who suffer. He stands on behalf of those that are oppressed. Not only do we serve a God of justice; we serve a God of compassion.

The word *compassion* comes from two root words meaning to "suffer with." To say that God has compassion on victims of poverty and injustice is to say that God actually suffers with them. We serve a compassionate God who responds to the needs of all people in every circumstance and gives to the point of sacrifice.

Read the following passages:
Deuteronomy 10:18
Deuteronomy 24:19
Jeremiah 22:3
Zechariah 7:9-10a

*Defend the cause of widow, fatherless, Gives food & clothing, reduce & sufferers. Do not shed innocent blood. Rescue the oppressed wrong-doer.*

What acts of real-world compassion are attributed to God? *Orphans*

*Administer true justice, show compassion & mercy to one another*

What acts of real-world compassion does God instruct His people to do? *Take care of each other. Take care of the less fortunate— aliens, widow + orphans. Rescue the oppressed*

Jesus, once again, showed us how to live a life of compassion by His example:

"Then Jesus went to all the towns and villages, teaching in their synagogues, preaching the good news of the kingdom, and healing every disease and every sickness. When He saw the crowds, He felt compassion for them, because they were weary and worn out, like sheep without a shepherd. Then He said to His disciples, 'The harvest is abundant, but the workers are few. Therefore, pray to the Lord of the harvest to send out workers into His harvest'" (Matthew 9:35-38).

Did Jesus see those with illness as an inconvenience? Did He look at them with disdain and attempt to find a way to avoid their suffering? No—His first response was compassion; He suffered with them. He met their needs by healing them of "every disease and sickness." He then "[summoned] His 12 disciples [and] gave them authority over unclean spirits, to drive them out and to heal every disease and sickness" (Matthew 10:1). He personally responded by healing *and* sending His followers to do the same.

Do you believe God still gets personally involved in the suffering of humanity as He did in and through the Person of Jesus?

How? *Through His Church. We are to be His hands and feet to a hurting + broken world. Love the unloved. Touch the untouched. Be the light in the darkness as Jesus was*

The last several statements regarding our response to suffering as Christ-followers might sound extreme. Read the parable of the Good Samaritan in Luke 10, starting in verse 23. Does the Samaritan's response seem extreme, too?

*— No. We are to treat each man as our brother — Because God is our Father & they are His children too ✓*

Perhaps we have the misconception that compassion is a purely emotional attribute. Real, biblical compassion is not just taking pity on someone. _Feeling badly is not compassion._ You cannot simply say, "I feel badly and wish I could do something." At best, this can be called sympathy; at worst, it is apathy. If we take God's compassion as the basis of our definition, we know that real compassion is both suffering alongside someone in pain and then _acting_ on that person's behalf. Because of His combination of presence and action, Jesus has been called "the suffering servant" and "the wounded healer."[5] He was not content to suffer and be wounded only; He took action by serving and healing.

Biblical compassion requires action.

> Do you believe that biblical compassion requires a personal and engaging response from _every_ believer? *Yes, John 13:15 Jesus set the perfect example for us to follow. His compassion led Him to be born in a manger, and also meant finally die on the cross.*
>
> Why or why not? *The Lord expects us to follow Jesus' example & be the change in the world. True compassion can be painful, at some points it will be painful.*
>
> Does biblical compassion differ from worldly compassion? *The world often feels bad & lets it go at that. If they are sufficiently moved they may give some money at the problem. But biblical compassion requires action - it requires us to get our hands dirty. We have to get involved. We are God's hands & feet to the world.*

Read these passages again noticing the present, ongoing language that God uses in these verses:

DEUTERONOMY 10:18
DEUTERONOMY 24:19-22
JEREMIAH 22:3
ZECHARIAH 7:9-10A

Write out the verbs in these passages. For example, write down "defends" and "loves" and "giving."

Every one of these statements calls for an ongoing response from us. These verses show that we are called to continue doing good as we are living our lives, not according to the convenience of the act but according to the need.

Your next questions might be, "Who am I supposed to be compassionate to? Should I be compassionate to and suffer with the believer before the unbeliever? What about the guy on the street corner? What about the person outside my country? What if a person doesn't have the same color of skin that I do? What am I supposed to do? In what order should I be compassionate?" *Everyone is your neighbor & your brother.*

The answer—as always—comes straight from God's Word. God tells us three important things about our response to suffering that might surprise some of us: 1) We should respond to the needs of people in all circumstances; 2) We should respond to the needs of anyone who needs help, even foreigners, even people outside of our fold; 3) We should give according to the needs of people to the point of our own sacrifice.

Jesus told a story to illustrate the nature of compassion in Luke 10. There are some interesting things going on in this parable that are important for us to understand. We know that the man who was robbed was coming from Jerusalem, so we can fairly safely assume he was Jewish. Yet two Jewish religious leaders (the priest and the Levite) chose not to help the man in need, though he was one of their own countrymen. The person who did stop was a Samaritan, which is significant considering that Jews and Samaritans were enemies. The Samaritan chose to "[love] those who hated him, [risk] his own life, [spend] his own money (two days' wages for a laborer), and was never publicly honored or rewarded as far as we know."[6]

Did the Samaritan concern himself with what was on his agenda before he encountered the man in need? Did the Samaritan excuse himself because of the race, social status, or wealth of the needy man? Far from it. In fact, the money the Samaritan gave to take care of the needy man was equal to about two days' pay. Does this sound like sacrifice to you? *Yes.* Here we find a man who responded to the need of another immediately, helped a foreigner, and gave to the point of sacrifice. The Samaritan shows us what it truly means to have compassion and illustrates beautifully the ministry of Jesus and those who follow Him.

Think about it: there was no logical reason that the Samaritan should have rearranged his schedule, put himself in danger, and given two days' wages to help a stranger. But apparently, compassion does not does not bow to logic. He gave for the same reason Jesus gave and the same reason Jesus wants us to give. We simply give because *we are givers*.

Do you usually need a reason to feel compassion?

*Not usually. — What I sometimes do is find reasons no to feel compassion. One example — this person is in a situation of their own creation due to their own sin — drug addiction selfishness etc. + so they don't deserve my help. That is of course, I didn't deserve Jesus' sacrifice on the cross.*

Why do you feel compassion is hard to find sometimes?

*Because it requires us to love & to reach out & to often be hurt to be spurned or rejected & see nothing come from our efforts.*

Are we, as Americans, too cynical or removed to feel biblical compassion?

*Often we are, yes. We have seen too many con men (and women) and don't want to be taken advantage of. We also expect the government to take care of the needy & hurting when it is so clearly the job of the Church*

As Christ ultimately gave of Himself even to the point of death on a cross, so we are called to pour out our time and resources indiscriminately on those around us so that people will see the love of Christ through our words and actions.

## RIGHTEOUSNESS

We not only serve a God of justice and compassion; we serve a God of righteousness. The following statement may sound strange at first, but this is the only way I can say it: we serve a God who is on His own side and on the side of those who are on His side. Read it again—we serve a God who's on His own side. He's also on the side of those who are on His side, doing the things He wants to accomplish, whatever those things may be. *Lord, I want to always be on your side.*

To put it more clearly, God does not come over to our team. If we choose to help those in need, we join His. Any time we act for the needy, for the oppressed, for those that need clothing, or for the imprisoned, we join God on the side He's already on.

Conversely, God is *not* on the side of those who are *not* on His side. Throughout the Bible, God judged and condemned those who perpetuated injustice. He enacted His righteous wrath time and time again on those who used their power and authority to take from the weak and the defenseless. Our God is a God who actually takes sides, gets righteously angry, and declares right from wrong.

How is God's emotional life different from our own?
How is it the same? He is infinite + finite. we are

He is sad + happy, rejoices + mourns
at the same time. He has not
limits. Sometimes we do physical,
emotional.
— He can feel the same things he
does in a limited, linear sense,
not all at the same time but
the same emotions.

Read each of the following passages and then write down the
words and phrases that describe what God was feeling in each of
these circumstances:

Isaiah 59:15b-16a — Displeased + astonished that there
was no one to intercede.
Jeremiah 5:28-29 — Did not — punish + avenge myself,
Amos 2:7-7a — standing on others the way of the humble
Zechariah 7:9-12b — He was angry because they
refused to pay attention + made their hearts like flint.

— Lord, I never want to displease,
disappoint or astonish You. I want to
make my Daddy proud of me.
— Let me not be known as someone who
did not act when others + suffered +
others needed me. Even if it is
hard or involves sacrifice let
me be someone who else.
— Let me never step on others to
advance myself.
— Let my heart be soft for Your things
o Lord.

Listen to "God of Justice"
by Tim Hughes on your
playlist. Is God's justice a
comfortable part of His
character for you?

David, Moses, the prophets, Jesus, and the apostles all describe God as a judge who has clearly made known right from wrong and is passionate about the difference. As we desire to imitate Christ, reflect the love of God, and live according to God's plan for our individual and collective lives, we must also learn right from wrong and then act according to our convictions. We must, that is, if we want to be on God's side. *it will be on your side.*

## GOD'S REAL WORLD RESPONSE

God's character consistently stirs Him to action. We serve a God who intervenes on behalf of the poor and the oppressed; He does not stand idly by. According to the Bible, God's justice, compassion, and moral clarity compel Him to an active real-world response. We don't find any hint in the Bible of a God who offers weightless sympathies, best wishes, or suggests that the atrocities perpetrated against people are some kind of character-building exercises.

It is true that God uses circumstances in our lives as tools to shape our character, but some things are so heinous, so terrible, that suggesting for a moment that they are "character builders" makes a mockery of human suffering. Is a child's character built when he dies slowly of malnutrition? How is a young girl's character built when she is sold as a sex slave? Do we look at a man who has lost his legs and an arm from the sharp blade of a machete in the Rwandan genocide and tell him, "You lost three limbs to build your character."? No. These are examples of grievous misuse of power, and they are to be stopped. I read in the Bible of a God who wants evildoers brought to account and the vulnerable people protected in the here and now, not the by and by.

## IN DEFENSE OF ALL THINGS ESSENTIAL

Some might argue that issues I've mentioned are better left in the political arena: "Let governments take care of physical needs, and let the church care for the soul," they might say. As an evangelist at heart, I affirm the supreme importance of world evangelization. The greatest task we are called to in this life is the salvation of "all nations" (Matthew 28:19). But in seeking the fulfillment of Jesus' commission to us, we must acknowledge that "our battle is not against flesh and blood, but against the rulers, against the authorities, against the world powers of this darkness, against the spiritual forces of evil in the heavens" (Ephesians 6:12).

As we have seen in the events of 9/11 and other atrocities around the world, the powers of darkness and the forces of evil manifest themselves on this earth as real hunger, real sickness, real nakedness, real slavery,

"Invisible Children" is a documentary about the child soldiers of Uganda. Find out more about how to host a viewing party at *www.invisiblechildren.com.*

real forced prostitution, real imprisonment, and real beating. Our battle for the soul makes it imperative that we engage the enemy on these fronts as well.

Gary Haugen expresses well the primacy of evangelism and the need to also meet the needs of those who are suffering: "While never, ever neglecting or subordinating spiritual needs, *which are primary,* Jesus always called His followers to respond to hunger with food, to nakedness with clothes, to imprisonment with visitation, to beatings with bandages and to injustice with justice."

James wrote, "If a brother or sister is without clothes and lacks daily food, and one of you says to them, 'Go in peace, keep warm, and eat well,' but you don't give them what the body needs, what good is it?" (James 2:15-16). The psalmist wrote, "LORD, who is like You, rescuing the poor from one too strong for him, the poor or the needy from one who robs him?" (Psalm 35:10b). Psalm 140:12 says, "I know that the LORD upholds the just cause of the poor, justice for the needy." Or how about Jeremiah 20:13: "Sing to the LORD! Praise the LORD, for He rescues the life of the needy from the hand of evil people."

Our primary call is to make disciples of all nations, baptize them, and teach them to obey God's commands. To draw them into a relationship with Jesus, baptize them according to His command, yet neglect the act of teaching them to obey all of God's commands, leaves out a major component of what it means to make disciples. True disciples follow all the commands of God that are so clearly revealed to us in Scripture. We are to share the gospel, baptize, *and* teach our fellow brothers and sisters to obey the entire counsel of God. We teach the commands of God by word *and* deed. Therefore, one of the greatest ways to evangelize the world is to live lives worthy of the calling of God through proclaiming the gospel while meeting the needs of those around us. The two are absolutely inseparable.

## GOD'S CHARACTER GIVES US OUR MARCHING ORDERS

Our response to poverty and injustice should not come from guilt we feel over the quantity or quality of our possessions. God desires that we be compelled by true, biblical compassion rather than guilt. He wants us to suffer with others and respond out of that shared suffering. He doesn't want us to take action based on a man-made sense of guilt or because giving to the poor and needy happens to be en vogue with the Hollywood elite and the men and women of the Forbes 400. Let compassion—and nothing else—move us to action.

I've seen what true compassion can create. We bore witness in 2005 to two of the largest physical tragedies of our day: Hurricane Katrina and the tsunami in Indonesia. Both of these events resulted in an outpouring of both local and international concern. At Frontline, where I am the teaching pastor, we were inundated with young adults calling and emailing our church staff to see what they could do to help in both these tragedies.

When Katrina hit the shores of Louisiana and the levees of New Orleans broke, people like you and I saw suffering and took action. In just a matter of days, teams were formed and deployed. People took vacation time to help in the area hit hardest. People left their families to go help hundreds of displaced families. They stayed and worked in some of the most difficult situations that any of them could imagine. They will tell you today that they wouldn't trade their suffering and sacrifice for anything because, through these experiences, they learned what it means to love with the love of Christ: to see a need and meet it based on the compassion that only God can supernaturally place in His children.

We saw a very similar response when the tsunami hit in Indonesia. Our phones rang off the hook with people asking what we as a Christian community were going to do to respond. Understand that these people weren't calling to make sure that the institutional church was responding by sending a check or making a formal statement to the press. No, these people were calling to see what we as children of God were doing and how they could personally and sacrificially join in God's work. These people were trying to find out where they could get involved to meet the needs of suffering people. The compassion that was expressed for Katrina victims in the United States was now being extended halfway around the world to those in need in Indonesia. The young adults of Frontline got it. God's compassion knows no borders, and neither did the compassion of the young adults at our church.

I was amazed at what happened next. God brought an amazing opportunity to our community. We were given an opportunity to help rebuild an Indonesian village. Supplies for homes had already been donated and teams were ready to build. Our part in God's plan involved raising $40,000 to purchase a piece of land.

As a part of our Katrina relief, the 20- and 30-year-olds at Frontline had already donated over $32,000. Could a group of young adults raise $72,000 in a matter of weeks? Could we replace our "need" for Starbucks with the true needs of others? Could we put our plans to buy a new car or a new television on hold so that we could give sacrificially to help others? Could we come together and do what none of us could do alone?

You bet we could . . . and we did. Not only did we collect money, but we sent numerous mission teams of young adults to the storm ravaged region of New Orleans.  We also sent a team of missionaries to serve the people of the village where we had already purchased the acreage for their new community. We sent a team of ambassadors for Christ to preach the good news of God's love and salvation through Jesus Christ! We "suffered with" the suffering people in that village and acted with compassion.

Read 1 Peter 1:13-16, 22-25. *Love one another from the heart, deeply.*

What has God taught you most about His character? *He loves the hurting & the broken. How many times does it talk about caring for the alien, widow & the fatherless. We must make that our priority as well.*

Now read Hebrews 4:12-13.

Has God judged the thoughts and attitudes of your heart and revealed any areas of your life that, at this point, don't match up to His standards of godly compassion? *Oh. Yes. Sometimes I am so selfish & I fail to love deeply & truly care about others. I know what I should do & I don't do it. Forgive me O God. I cry for the hurting & broken - hunger kids, single mothers, foster children, kids in Uganda.*

# STUDY

"For the word of God is living and effective and sharper than any two-edged sword, penetrating as far as to divide soul, spirit, joints, and marrow; it is a judge of the ideas and thoughts of the heart" (Hebrews 4:12-13).

This week, try embracing what God has placed into your hands in the form of the Bible. Sometimes we just read the Bible like it's a textbook to get through. As you read this week, do more—dwell, think, imagine, believe, and change.

**For the next six days,** read one chapter a day of the book of Philippians. But do more than read it; read a verse, and put it down. Think about it. Journal your thoughts before continuing. Try and get in the habit of doing more than *tasting* the Word; *ingest* it in significant chunks. On the seventh day, journal about your experience as a whole. Has anything changed in you during the week? Have your attitudes begun to be transformed? Did you see things you did not know were there?

NAME: **JEFF KILLEBREW**

JOB OR MINISTRY: **DESIRE STREET MINISTRIES, NEW ORLEANS**

**WWW.DESIRESTREET.ORG**

# NEIGHBORHOOD BY NEIGHBORHOOD

For the better part of the past nine years, Jeff Killebrew found himself in inner city New Orleans—on Desire Street to be exact. "Desire Street used to be the second largest public housing development in the country," Jeff says. "By the early '90s, HUD rated the Desire Project the 'worst community in the nation.' Take all the stereotypical inner-city statistics, multiply them a few times over, and that was the nature of the area. Children under 18 were the majority of the population—the vast majority growing up without fathers and under the poverty line."

The mission was clear-cut—revitalize the Desire neighborhood through spiritual and community development. With their focus on youth, they provided safe recreational opportunities, tutoring, and Bible studies. In doing so, they became fathers to the fatherless. "We called our philosophy 'incarnational ministry,' so we lived in the community and became neighbors, integrating ourselves as much as possible into the fabric of the community," Jeff explains.

Immersed in the work of Desire Street Ministries, he and his roommates learned firsthand what it was like to grow up in this area. "Poverty is relative, and it's not always about financial means. Poverty is pervasive and affects housing, economic development, educational opportunities, and a whole slew of other issues. That's why our organization was holistic in its approach to transforming young lives," Jeff says.

As for rewarding work ... well, Jeff has a different perspective. "Working to help people overcome poverty and injustice appears to be rewarding because it has meaning and purpose, and that it does. Our ministry in New Orleans was not a quick-fix kind of program," he stresses. "I was in it for the long haul, and the rewards were often slow in coming. You could find joy and reward in the small victories but always had to readjust to a long-term focus and see things from God's point of view to not get discouraged with slow progress. When you're trying to transform lives and communities, it'll probably be three generations before the damage done by the previous three has been reversed.

"The most rewarding thing has been my own personal growth that came as a result of the challenge of being called to this kind of work. It shatters preconceived ideas—some of them anyway," Jeff says. It stretched him to a greater dependence on God as well as the opportunity to make friends and become neighbors with people that a more traditional, comfortable lifestyle would have not afforded him. "That's the real reward," Jeff adds.

There is, however, one glaring misconception—the idea that ministry to the poor is for the select few and not central to the call of every Christian gets under Jeff's skin. "I learned that righting wrongs and serving those in need is at the very heart of Christ's ministry and, in fact, the heart of God," he says. "Not everyone is called to move into the inner city or give up the security of a corporate job, but every Christian should get his or her hands dirty in the struggle in some form or fashion.

"The Bible teaches that being a disciple of Christ means we are supposed to share in His sufferings," Jeff continues. "Christians should take action against injustice because that reflects the love of Christ. Open doors for the gospel part of living for Him will also mean suffering to further the cause of the Gospel. My experiences have increased my understanding of how big and loving and merciful and forgiving God is. I view the sacrifice of Christ differently and therefore see my role differently. He died that we, that I, might find life in Him. And with that eternal reward comes earthly responsibility. Luke 9:23-24 speaks to that truth, that calling."

"THEN HE SAID TO [THEM] ALL, 'IF ANYONE WANTS TO COME WITH ME, HE MUST DENY HIMSELF, TAKE UP HIS CROSS DAILY, AND FOLLOW ME. FOR WHOEVER WANTS TO SAVE HIS LIFE WILL LOSE IT, BUT WHOEVER LOSES HIS LIFE BECAUSE OF ME WILL SAVE IT.'" — LUKE 9:23-24

# THE TRUE CONDITION OF OUR WORLD

I walked into LaSoya's restaurant in San Antonio, Texas, just before 9 a.m. to hang out with my good friend, Doug Miller. We met weekly for breakfast tacos and coffee at a restaurant owned by his twin cousins, Danny and David LaSoya. My wife was just a few days from having our second child—a little girl we would name Katherine McKenna Phillips. We celebrated my son Parker's second birthday only two months before, and we had just moved into a beautiful house in a gated community with our backyard buttressing up to a green belt behind our house. Life was good. I was living warm and cozy inside my American cocoon.

I remember, though, the exact moment my cocoon began to unravel (never to be spun again). I sat down with Doug and caught a glimpse of a strange and surreal picture on the thirteen inch color television screen sitting atop the soft drink cooler in the corner of the restaurant. The volume was down too low to hear anything, but I could clearly see the Twin Towers in New York City. One had smoke billowing out from all sides near the top of the building. I didn't know what was going on, but somehow I knew everything was different than it had been half an hour earlier. But just how different?

For the creation eagerly waits with anticipation for God's sons to be revealed. For the creation was subjected to futility—not willingly, but because of Him who subjected it—in the hope that the creation itself will also be set free from the bondage of corruption into the glorious freedom of God's children.

**ROMANS 8:19-21**

# THE TRUE CONDITION OF OUR WORLD

**WAKE-UP CALL**

Everyone in the restaurant had turned to watch that little screen in disbelief. Then it happened—live, right there in front of us all, a commercial jet slammed into the South Tower of the World Trade Center causing a terrifyingly huge explosion. "Oh my God, the second tower has just been hit by another plane. I can't believe what I'm seeing!" exclaimed the announcer. None of us could.

I looked at Doug, he looked at me, and we both got up and walked out of the restaurant. I called my wife who was still sleeping and said, "I'm coming home right now. Turn on the television. The Twin Towers have both been hit. I know this sounds crazy, honey, but I think we're at war. Call your mom right now! I'll be there in five minutes."

My wife's mom was working at the White House in the East Wing at the visitor's center at the time, but had been home for a few days helping us prepare for the birth of our second child. I wanted to know if she could find out anything more than what was being reported on the news.

When I arrived at home a few minutes later I saw footage of the Pentagon in flames and I was absolutely certain at that point that there would be dozens more of these strikes throughout the day—the White House, the Capitol, Sears Tower—had World War III really started? What was I going to do to protect my pregnant wife and 2-year-old boy? Maybe I could send them to the Kirk family house in Kerrville, Texas. That was probably far enough away from a big city to be safe. People were going to be looking for guidance, prayer, counsel. What was the church going to do?

We all know now that there were no more buildings destroyed that day, and, arguably, World War III did not begin. No invasion forces landed on our shores; no paratroopers fell from the sky. That didn't change the fact that everyone's cocoon had been ferociously ripped open. Nothing in life would be the same. The world was now different. We were no longer safe. For me, September 11, 2001, was the day that the true condition of the world kicked me in the gut.

My second child, Katherine, was born on September 14, 2001, literally in the shadow of a hospital television set with video footage of the Twin

Towers and the Pentagon playing over and over; with political analysts debating what our response should be as a nation even before we knew who or what we should respond to. We watched the prayer service with Billy Graham presiding. There I was, a father of two, celebrating the birth of my second beautiful child at the same time being unable to keep my mind from trying to process what kind of world our children had been born into.

The world became very big, very evil, and very cold that day. The scales fell from my eyes over the next several months. I felt as though I was waking from a blissful sleep and was being accosted by the grim reality of the world before I even had a chance to focus my eyes from slumber. I remember thinking, "What am I supposed to do as a Christ-follower, preacher, and evangelist to respond to this 'new' world?"

## HAD ANYTHING REALLY CHANGED?

From a global perspective, very little changed on September 11, 2001. The U.S. was simply baptized into the cruel and ongoing battle of oppressive evil that has plagued our world since the fall of man. The difference now was that our walls had been breached and we had been attacked on our own soil—an unthinkable event for most of us. We were victims of catastrophic evil in our own backyard. This was nothing new to the nation of Rwanda where 800,000 were slaughtered in just seven years before 9/11, or to those who witnessed 2,000,000 murders under the Pol Pot regime in Cambodia from 1975 to 1979, or the survivors of the Holocaust who witnessed the annihilation of 6,000,000 of their friends and family, or the murder of 7,000,000 people by forced famine under Stalin's dictatorship for 2 years in 1932 and 1933. At long last, the ongoing war of good and evil became very, very visible to our side of the world.

People from all over the United States flooded churches, synagogues, and mosques for several weeks after 9/11. Tragically, those same people, at least in the Christian churches, filed out almost as quickly as they stampeded in. They were looking for assurance, hope, help, compassion, and understanding—they came looking for God, but by their actions proclaimed that they had not found Him at church. Fear and uncertainty over the events of 9/11 were coupled with hopelessness and doubt as the church seemingly could not provide what people were looking for.

Listen to "Tanzania" by Alli Rogers from your playlist. Do you find yourself living in an Americanized coccoon?

We in the American church have been so insulated from the suffering of our world that when unspeakable evil breached our walls we did not know how to respond. The church—God's agent for change in the world—responded largely with platitudes from the pulpit and inactivity in the streets when the world needed us most. [8]

### RAW, HOPELESS, STRICKEN . . . BUT TRUE

Two billion people live on less than $2 a day. That's one-third of the people on our planet. In the tsunami that hit Indonesia in the fall of 2004, 250,000 people died. The same number dies every 40 days of AIDS in sub-Saharan Africa alone. Think of it like this: more than 9 "AIDS tsunamis" will hit sub-Saharan Africa this year alone.

At least 1,836 died as a result Hurricane Katrina's landfall in New Orleans and the Mississippi gulf coast. The numbers could be higher. Yet the same number dies every 46 minutes from lack of clean water—lack of clean water! Put another way, in less than the time of the average church service, 1,300 people will die around the world because their water is dirty. Some research suggests that $8 billion would be sufficient to take on the task of providing clean water for every human being on the planet.

Here's a statistic that's closer to home: nearly 3,000 people died in the Twin Towers, the Pentagon, and Flight 93 on 9/11. It was a horrible tragedy for our country, but that same number of people were slaughtered *every* 8 hours of *every* day for 100 days in the Rwanda genocide in 1994. The body count reached 800,000 before the murders ceased. The Rwandan genocide had the same effect as the tragedy of 9/11 happening at 8 a.m., again at 4 p.m., and then again at midnight every day for three and a half months.

### WE OWE IT ALL TO ADAM . . . AND EVE

Each of us must come to terms with the true condition of our world. Reality is not accurately reflected in the well-manicured suburbs of our culture. It is not even really seen in the slums of our major U.S. cities. In reality, the slums of Los Angeles, Chicago, or Washington D.C., are virtual paradises compared to the conditions in which two-thirds of the people on the earth live. To begin to understand this is to begin to peer through the well-woven fabric of our isolated cocoon and see with our own eyes and feel with our own hearts the unimaginable suffering and injustice that is commonplace in two-thirds of our world.

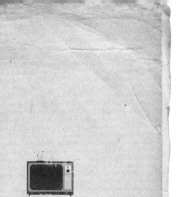

"God Grew Tired of Us" is the documentary account of three of the "Lost Boys" of Sudan who escaped their war torn homeland. The film chronicles their struggle in establishing new lives while remaining connected their past.

CHECK OUT
*www.godgrewtiredofus.com* for more information about this important movie.

Read the following passages:
Psalm 19:8
Matthew 13:15
Isaiah 6:9
Ephesians 1:18

What do these passages tell you about the connection God has created between the eyes and the heart?

Why is this connection necessary for God to work in the world?

So what is the real condition of our world at large? What's truly happening around the globe? How do we look holistically at the world in such a way as to come to terms with the best approach for our involvement? First, we must understand that the condition of our world today is a continuation of what began when Eve "took some of [the tree's] fruit and ate it" and then offered the fruit to Adam who seemed to be more than willing to partake himself (Genesis 3:6). The condition of the world is the result of sin entering the world through Adam and Eve.

The suffering we now see and the injustice that permeates our societies is not a recent reality brought on by oppressive politicians, radical religious factions around the world, or by soccer moms driving gas-guzzling SUVs. Neither can we blame it on globalization or the large debt loads of poverty stricken third world countries. All of these are nothing more than symptoms of the true culprit—sin.

It's very important to understand that the result of sin on humanity was both physical and spiritual. Adam's sin literally changed everything for all of us, and no one is free from the devastating effects of sin when we are born into the world. The condition of the world today can be explained by one three letter word—sin.

If sin is the true culprit, then every issue of poverty, injustice, and oppression has a *spiritual* element to it. The problems of our world are not just political, racial, economic, or philosophical issues (or a combination of any of these). Therefore, we can't solve these symptomatic problems without first tackling the problem of sin. Our working assumption then for our study is this: without spiritual transformation we will never have social transformation.

Before sin entered the world, Adam and Eve lived in the Garden of Eden, where they had communication with God and the pleasure of direct contact with Him each day. They existed in a blissful relationship with God that was meant to last forever—no death; no suffering; no injustice. The only thing they weren't supposed to do was eat from that tree. Everything else was available to them. But when Adam and Eve decided to make a choice against God's plan, they were banished from the garden and both sin and death entered our world. As a result, our world became warped and damaged. We now live in a fallen world full of fallen people.

Because God is just, He punished Adam and all of creation in response to sin. God said in Genesis 3:

**"Because you listened to your wife's voice and ate from the tree about which I commanded you, 'Do not eat from it': The ground is cursed because of you. You will eat from it by means of painful labor all the days of your life. It will produce thorns and thistles for you, and you will eat the plants of the field. You will eat bread by the sweat of your brow until you return to the ground, since you were taken from it. For you are dust, and you will return to dust" (Genesis 3:17-19).**

We're all born into this sin, and we all suffer the consequences of God's judgment. This wasn't just a spiritual spanking and it didn't just affect Adam and Eve. The effects of sin are experienced in every part of creation.

Read Romans 8:18-23.

How does creation pay the price of sin entering our world?

**Listen to "It's Not Political" before your group gets together to discuss this session. (Your group leader will send it to you via email.)**

**How can you separate your awareness and commitment regarding these issues from a particular political ideology?**

Write down the key results of sin on creation.

Romans 8:19-22 states the reality of the world's condition:

**"The *creation* waits in eager expectation for the sons of God to be revealed. For the *creation* was subjected to frustration, not by its own choice, but by the will of the one who subjected it, in hope that the *creation* itself will be liberated from its bondage to decay and brought into the glorious freedom of the children of God. We know that the whole *creation* has been groaning as in the pains of childbirth right up to the present time"** *(emphasis added).*

As we read this passage carefully we realize that creation is paying a price for the sin of man. Like man, the world is subject to decay and to death. Reflect again on the key words that we find inside this one passage: pain, suffering, bondage, decay, frustration. Some versions of the Bible will include "futility" in this passage. God's creation is in the throws of agony. All the world—not just humanity—is experiencing frustration, bondage, and decay.

In the throws of its deterioration, creation is actually waiting for the redemption of God's children. I think verse 20 is absolutely amazing.

**"For the creation was subject to frustration, not by its own choice, but by the will of the one who subjected it, in the hope that creation itself will be liberated from bondage and decay and be brought into the glorious freedom of the children of God."**

When Christ comes again in all His glory to redeem His church, all of creation will be redeemed with it

In fact, in Revelation 21, God tells us "a new heaven and new earth" will be created to take the place of "the first heaven and the first earth" which will have "passed away" (Revelation 21:1). What an incredibly exciting truth! Just as creation along with humanity fell into decay because of sin, when the people of God are redeemed, creation will also be restored to what God has always planned for it to be.

### IN THE MEANTIME

So what happens in the meantime? What are we supposed to be doing as the people of God until Christ comes again to redeem His church and all of creation? We are called to do two essential things: announce the good news of the coming of the kingdom of God and salvation through Jesus Christ, and provide signs of God's coming redemption by doing the good works that God has prepared in advance for us to do (Ephesians 2:10).

Until that final redemption at Christ's return, we're commanded to go out and spread the word: the Lord is coming. Redemption is at hand, and we can all be reconciled to God through the saving work of Jesus Christ. While we proclaim this message verbally, we are to prove its validity through our commitment to bringing about the characteristics of the kingdom we are announcing. Until Jesus redeems creation, it is left to the people of God to offer signs of the kingdom of God. We do so by feeding people, clothing people, and providing for their needs.

For a continuing conversation about the link between evangelism and social action take a look at *Revolution and Renewal* by Tony Campolo and Bruce Main.

In Matthew 9 and 10, Jesus built His team of 12 disciples and called them to a life of ministry. He then sent them out with their first ministry assignment:

**"As you go, announce this: 'The kingdom of heaven has come near.' Heal the sick, raise the dead, cleanse those with skin diseases, drive out demons. You have received free of charge; give free of charge" (Matthew 10:7-8).**

Jesus was extremely specific and His instructions were simple: preach the kingdom of God and do good works while you are preaching. Preach the kingdom. Do good works. That's it.

Later, because Philip " . . . proclaimed the good news about the kingdom of God and the name of Jesus Christ, both men and women were baptized" (Acts 8:12). A large gathering of people believed in Jesus because Philip went out and proclaimed both the coming kingdom of God and the name of Christ. That is, he proclaimed the redemption of all creation and the opportunity to have a personal relationship with the God of the universe through Jesus.

Paul too carried out this important ministry: "After arranging a day with him, many came to him at his lodging." A crowd came to the place where Paul was staying, and " . . . from dawn to dusk he expounded and witnessed about the kingdom of God. He persuaded them concerning Jesus from both the Law of Moses and the Prophets" (Acts 28:23).

Paul spent the entire day preaching about the coming kingdom of God and the name of Jesus Christ by whom all men can be saved. We're called to spread the same two-sided message. When Christ comes again, all of us who have accepted Jesus Christ as our Lord and Savior will be ushered into this long-awaited kingdom of God. *Until then, through both word and deed, we are to give witness to God's love to a lost world.*

*Do you see it?*

I read a story a few years back that I think describes well our responsibility to the world around us. Several climbers were being rescued from the side of a mountain. The rescue helicopter was only able to reach each man one at a time because they had fallen on different areas of the mountain. As the helicopter and the rescue team got to each man, they would lower a rescuer down to that individual. That rescuer would go down and administer basic first aid—water, bandages, food and medicine—and would also announce the ultimate rescue that was to come.

He would say something like, "Fred, here's food and water, and here's medical aid, but this is just the beginning of things to come. You're about to be removed from your present situation and taken to another place. We're going to take you away from this place so you won't be cold any longer. You won't be hurt any longer. You won't be thirsty or hungry. The helicopter has a few more people to save before they get to you, but I've been sent to take care of your needs and to assure you that they're coming."

That is a picture of the church's role. We're the ones in the helicopter. We're the rescuers. We've been given the message. We have the ability to go out and feed, clothe, and give medical attention and water. We can go into these situations of crisis, be lowered down from the rescue helicopter to individuals, feed them, clothe them, care for them, and say, "Listen, this is only the beginning. This is just a taste of things to come. One day the kingdom of God is coming to redeem all those who have started a relationship with Jesus. I can show you how you can have a relationship with Him, because He sent me to take care of your needs. One day soon you'll see Him face to face; we just have to pick up a few more people before we go home."

We have been given a special invitation from God; a mission that only the people of God can accomplish. The very mission of the church is to go out among the dying, the hurt, and the needy, and share the good news of salvation in Jesus through word and deed.

God's plan is to use us to provide for the immediate needs of people. Through the service and sacrifice of the people of God, the gospel is proclaimed to a world in agony. As Gary Haugan often says, the church is God's "Option A" and He doesn't have an "Option B."

Are we as the people of God, at least in the United States, abdicating our role as God's agent for change in the world?

How does this affect the big picture of God's plan to redeem the world?

# SPEAK

Information is power. If that is true, then you have the potential to be an incredibly powerful force for the kingdom of God . . . if you get the information.

**Watch the news this week**, but watch it with purpose. Pay particular attention to stories relating to poverty, suffering, and justice. After you watch the news, spend a little time on the internet to get the back story of what you have just seen. Then take the next step: during at least one conversation this week bring up the issue you examined. Talk about what you learned, but just as importantly, listen to someone else's perspective without judging it.

Take this chance to begin meaningful dialogue that will lead to prayer, transformation, and action.

NAME: **JOHN KOON**

JOB OR MINISTRY: **MISSIONARY**

**CHILDREN'S EMERGENCY RELIEF INTERNATIONAL**

**CHISINAU, MOLDOVA**

# SEEKING FREEDOM AND JUSTICE. HERE. NOW.

Moldova—most people haven't heard of the Eastern European country, much less ventured to travel there. Yet in this tiny country, John Koon has found a big calling. John serves with Children's Emergency Relief International, a faith-based humanitarian aid organization, working primarily with orphaned children. John organizes sponsorship and foster care relationships for children, teaches English at an orphanage, mentors teenagers, and finds himself looking injustice in the eye on a near daily basis.

"The most rewarding aspect of working in Moldova for me is the relationships I have with the kids at the orphanage," he says. "God has taught me so much through their perspective. It's been humbling for me to be embraced as a friend by these children whose culture is so vastly different from my own. Cross-cultural friendships are always challenging, but I believe that they are one of the most deeply rewarding experiences we can have."

While John loves the work he's found in Moldova, the culture can sometimes get the best of him. "I'm learning how to be a student of Moldovan culture—to live my daily life in this culture with humility. Humility and open-mindedness are essential for anyone engaging in cross-cultural relationships or ministry, and this has been hard for me because I've encountered and have been faced with the ugliness and brokenness of my own culture," John says. "But at the same time, in the midst of the struggle, I am learning more of what it means for me to embrace my ethnic and cultural identity as part of who God has created me to be, to claim the positive aspects of my culture, and to seek reconciliation and justice as I live in relationship with others."

But perhaps what drives John is his perspective on injustice. "I think that it is impossible to separate social justice from the gospel," John stresses. "My whole life I heard that Jesus came to save me from my personal sin, but I rarely heard that He also came to redeem entire societies from structural and institutional sin. From racism to economic injustice to sex slavery to hatred and war, our world is full of societal sin from which Jesus came to set us free.

"And as I've begun to realize these things, I've been overwhelmed not knowing how to begin to be a part of this movement Jesus started," he says. "So I decided to take the first step by following His call to Moldova and by being open to what He is teaching me here. I am daily faced with the reality of poverty, sex slavery, abuse, and neglect; and so I wrestle with these issues and seek to know how God is moving to bring freedom and justice. Here. Now.

"By breaking out of our 'gated communities' and living in friendship and community cross-culturally with the poor and with the outcast, we find the presence of Jesus in a whole new and profound way. We speak and breathe and live His love, which testifies that the God of the universe has not forgotten those whom society deems unworthy. Jesus lived His life among the rejected and the outcast of society, and I believe that we are called to follow Him into such a life," John says. "It is here that we will find His heart of compassion, His healing presence, and will somehow know more of what He meant when He said, 'whatever you did for one of the least of these brothers of Mine, you did for Me' (Matthew 25:40)."

And while he lives among injustice, John claims this truth: "The LORD executes acts of righteousness and justice for all the oppressed" (Psalm 103:6). "God's justice for the oppressed is a direct and tangible outpouring of His love and grace—His Spirit does these things, not any of us out of our own will or desire," he says.

---

"SEEK JUSTICE, ENCOURAGE THE OPPRESSED. DEFEND THE CAUSE OF THE FATHERLESS, PLEAD THE CASE OF THE WIDOW." — ISAIAH 1:17

# WHAT'S MY ROLE?

We can make a profound difference both in this life and in the "age to come" (Mark 10:30). While the task before us looks overwhelming, we know God has called each one of us "for good works, which God prepared ahead of time so that we should walk in them" (Ephesians 2:10). God has works of kindness, generosity, and compassion for us to do that are uniquely suited for our specific gifts and talents, and when accomplished in concert with all of our fellow believers, can collectively change the world. God's design is that we, the church—not the government, Hollywood, or big business—would be the agent of change in the world.

No one can do everything, but everyone can do *something* . . .

For the creation eagerly waits with anticipation for God's sons to be revealed. For the creation was subjected to futility—not willingly, but because of Him who subjected it—in the hope that the creation itself will also be set free from the bondage of corruption into the glorious freedom of God's children.

ROMANS 8:19-21

# WHAT'S MY ROLE?

### AMBASSADORS

The church is meant to be the agent of change for this suffering world because we are the only community that has the message of hope in Jesus Christ to accompany our acts of kindness and compassion.

This task is what God is committed to, and as His representatives, we must be committed to it as well.

Paul agreed with that assessment. In a passage that many biblical scholars say is the defining passage of his ministry, Paul tried to help the Christ-followers in the city of Corinth understand their role in God's plan. In so doing, he used a very specific word to explain exactly what God had invited him (and us) to be and do:

**"Now everything is from God, who reconciled us to Himself through Christ and gave us the ministry of reconciliation: that is, in Christ, God was reconciling the world to Himself, not counting their trespasses against them, and He has committed the message of reconciliation to us.** *Therefore, we are ambassadors for Christ;* **certain that God is appealing through us, we plead on Christ's behalf, 'Be reconciled to God'" (2 Corinthians 5:18-20,** *emphasis added***).**

Define "ambassador" in your own words.

Define "reconciliation" in your own words.

What do you think God want us to do as ministers of reconciliation?

We read in verse 18 that God "reconciled us to Himself through Christ and gave us the ministry of reconciliation." Every follower of Christ is part of this ministry of reconciliation. Essentially, reconciliation is God's initiative in Christ whereby He does not count men's sins against them. He has committed to us the message of His goal to bring humanity into right relationship with Himself.

Although we were enemies with God, we are now reconciled—in right relationship with God—because of Jesus' redemptive act on the cross. Our ministry of reconciliation, then, is inviting others to receive this gift of reconciliation with God through the redemptive work of Christ.

God has entrusted us with the most important message in the world. He has given us the privilege and responsibility to share the *only* message that can solve the world's sin problem.

It is because of this ministry that " . . . we are *ambassadors* for Christ; certain that God is appealing through us, we plead on Christ's behalf, 'Be reconciled to God'" (2 Corinthians 5:20).

As followers *of* Christ we are also ambassadors *for* Christ; we are to speak and act on His behalf. The dictionary definition of an ambassador is "a diplomatic agent of the highest rank accredited to a foreign government or sovereign, as the resident representative of his own government or sovereign, appointed for a special and often temporary diplomatic assignment."

An ambassador is a man or woman living in a foreign kingdom for the purpose of speaking or acting on behalf of the sovereign leader of his or her home kingdom or nation. The position is diplomatic in nature and is often a temporary assignment. In every sense, then, we are called to be ambassadors for Christ. We're on temporary assignment to speak and act on behalf of Christ, in His stead, until He comes again in glory.

Matthew Henry's commentary gives a similar explanation of Christian ambassadorship: "Believers come as ambassadors in God's name and act in Christ's stead *doing the very thing He did when He was on the earth and what He wills to be done now that He's in heaven"* [10]

Since I moved to the Washington D.C. area I've had the opportunity to talk with lobbyists, diplomats, congressmen, secret service agents . . . and ambassadors. One of the things that I've come to understand is that

Listen to "Do *Something*" before your group gets together to discuss this session. (Your group leader will send it to you via email.) What's the first step for you?

ambassadors are not hired to summarize the president's words or to do "something similar to" what the president desires to be done, much less give their own opinion. In fact, they are to do only two things: speak in the president's stead the *exact* words of the president and to act in the president's stead doing *exactly* what the he would do if he were there himself.

In the very same way, we are all called to be Christ's ambassadors. We are to do, as Henry wrote, "the very thing He did on the earth and what He wills to be done now that He's in heaven." We don't need to think of new ideas or a different message. We have been given the words to say and the good works to do; they should be the same things Jesus would say and do Himself if He were here.

Jesus said as much in John 20:21: "Peace to you! As the Father has sent Me, *I also send you" (emphasis added).* In the same way that God the Father sent Jesus down to the earth to do the good works and to preach the good news of the coming kingdom, Jesus is sending us out. He is sending us out to do the very same things He did. Don't get too creative—just go preach the gospel and do good as the hands and feet of Jesus Christ.

At our essence as believers, we can either be *proclaiming servers or serving proclaimers.* There is really not much difference in the two; both express the same truth. In either case, we shouldn't be proclaiming Christ without serving people, and we shouldn't be serving people without proclaiming Christ.

It's pretty simple if you think about it. *Our acts of service add credibility to the gospel message, while the message clarifies the purpose for our acts of service.* Do you see it? When we go out and do the things that Christ did when He walked the earth we're validating the message that we speak; the message we speak gives the reason for our actions. Service and evangelism are two sides of the same coin. Unfortunately, at least in this country, many churches preach the name of Jesus but are relatively uninvolved in serving those who are suffering. On the other side, there are organizations committed to social change, but silent regarding the name of Christ in the midst of their service. Jesus wants us to bridge the gap and be both.

### NOW WHAT?

What are the first steps that each of us can take to be part of changing the world through evangelism and service? Maybe you expect me to challenge you to respond by selling your possessions and moving to sub-Saharan Africa or leaving your job and go into "full-time ministry." Maybe you should, but I can't tell you that. I don't pretend to know what God wants specifically for you. While the details of our unique responses will be between each one of us and God, I can say with certainty that if we fail to understand and then incorporate some general practices into our lives then we'll be ignoring the most powerful tools of transformation—both personal transformation and social transformation—at our disposal. My prayer is that you will see the following practices, or disciplines, from a new perspective in light of what God has revealed to you so far in relation to the marriage of service and evangelism.

## GOD-SIZED PRAYER

First, there is always prayer—specifically, *intercession*. Intercessory prayer simply means prayer on behalf of other people. God calls us to bring everything to Him. Pray for our own needs, our own issues, and our own concerns—that's wonderful. But we should also get beyond ourselves and begin to pray on behalf of others.

In writing to the church of his day, James asked in James 5:13: "Are any among you suffering?"—perfect for our study, huh?—"He should pray." Isn't that interesting? He didn't tell them anything else but to pray.

When James got to the issue of suffering, he did not try to explain the pain of life with a big treatise or dissertation. His answer to the issue of suffering was not necessarily "knowing why;" it was prayer. Prayer is elemental. Prayer is the very well from which we draw the strength of Christ. Prayer is a foundational reality of what we're to do on the issues of suffering especially when we begin to understand the *spiritual* source of the *physical* suffering in our world.

Verse 14 says, "Is anyone among you sick? He should call for the elders of the church, and they should pray over him after anointing him with olive oil in the name of the Lord." Verse 15, "The prayer of faith will save the sick person, and the Lord will raise him up; and if he has committed sins, he will be forgiven."

The first thing we're called to do is pray and to pray with an understanding of the magnitude of God. Maybe this is where some of us are having trouble. Perhaps our view of God is just too small.

James 5 is a great passage that provides an example of all the ways in which God wants us to include prayer into our daily lives.

Write a short summary of this passage in your own words.

Is prayer something you incorporate enough into your life in light of this passage in James?

What do your prayers reveal about your view of God?

How does the God of your prayer life match up to the God of the Bible?

Recently, my wife and I were continuing our ongoing conversation about prayer. It's been a difficult discussion because prayer in our lives has been an up-and-down thing. I pray as a part of my ministry. I pray for my family. I do things in private, and then my wife and I have times of prayer with each other. We've had discussions, not of whether or not we *should* pray—that's not the issue—but what we're supposed to be praying about.

Around the time of this particular discussion, we put our house on the market. So we prayed, "God, please sell our house." Good thing to pray, right? God exhorts us not to "worry about anything, but in everything, through prayer and petition with thanksgiving, let your requests be made known to God" (Philippians 4:6).

The sale of our house certainly fell within the "everything" category so we prayed diligently about it. One night, after Julie and I prayed for our house to sell, I went up to put my two daughters, Katherine and Raney Grace, to bed. After they were down I told them it was time to pray. I put both my hands together, and they put their hands together. I said, "Do you guys want to say anything?" Raney, our 2-year-old, mumbled incoherently (because she can't talk very well) and then said, "Amen." Then Katherine said, "Yeah, I want to pray, Daddy."

I wrote this down just so I would get it exactly right. She said, "I pray for all the people in the world that they have food and don't get burnt by hot lava." (I think she probably watches too much of the Discovery Channel with her daddy). The first thing Katherine's prayer made me think was, "That is so cute! That is so darling, a little 4-year-old praying for all the people of the world to have food and not get burnt by hot lava. How sweet. I can't wait to tell Julie."

I finished praying with the girls and walked out of the room shutting the door behind me. Then I stopped. It was as though God said, "Todd, just a few minutes ago, you were praying for your house to get sold. When you did the angels looking down at you said to each other, 'Todd just prayed such a cute prayer. That is so sweet! Gabriel, did you catch that one? Can God sell his house . . . that's precious!' Then, when your 4-year-old daughter prayed 'for all the people in the world,' My entire heavenly host poised, waiting for My word to go into action. 'We finally got a God-sized prayer! Get food to the people in greatest need through the children of God! Redirect that lava flow in Hawaii! Get ready to move!'"

It's good and right to bring all our requests to God, whether our prayers are for a new job, the sale of a house, a raise, or even for God to bring us the right spouse. In addition to these prayers, however, we are instructed to intercede on behalf of others. My daughter understands this about prayer. She prayed for everyone in the world!

How would God respond to millions of people praying God-sized, humanly impossible prayers? What if we all began to pray, "God I know there's a lot of stuff out there, and it's overwhelming at least to me, and it even seems sometimes like there's nothing that we can do. But you make it really clear in the Bible that I (and everyone else) can do all things through Christ who strengthens each one of us. You want to use Your children to be the agents of change for this lost and suffering world. You desire that *none* should perish and that *all* would be saved. You hate injustice and oppression and the abuse of power. So these are my prayers: I ask You—because I believe in who You are and what You can do—save *everyone*. Stop the suffering. Lead us out to do the things that You have prepared for us to do. God, here I am; send me. Change the world through me and others like me."

Are we praying God-sized prayers, or are we just asking God to fix the things in our lives that make us uncomfortable? Have we lost that sense of wonder and certainty about God that a 4-year-old might have? Are we praying for big things that only God can do?

### ONLY GOD CAN GIVE US PASSION FOR THOSE IN NEED
Poverty, hopelessness, and despair give off a distinct aroma. The air becomes thick with the stench of hopelessness. I can usually discern who has prayed for the love of God to flow through them and who has not when I travel overseas because those who have not prayed for God to work through them and are trying in vain to serve in their own strength

Let go of all inhibitions, fears, and doubts, and write down a God-sized prayer about anything relating to anyone else but you. Continue to meditate on it over the next few days.

are repelled by the smell. But those who are empowered by the Spirit seem to be attracted by that same smell of hopelessness and despair as though it is a homing device guiding them to the places and people of greatest need.

We must pray for God to compel us to move toward the misery and hopelessness. We will not want to go there based on our own capacity for love and compassion; we must pray for God to give us His heart, His eyes, His nose, and His ears to experience people the way that Jesus experienced them in Matthew 9:35-36: "Jesus went through all the towns and villages, teaching in their synagogues, preaching the good news of the kingdom and healing every disease and sickness. When he saw the crowds, he had *compassion* on them, because they were harassed and helpless, like sheep without a shepherd. Then he said to his disciples, 'The harvest is plentiful but the workers are few. Ask the Lord of the harvest, therefore, to send out workers into his harvest field'" *(emphasis added)*.

If we fail to pray for a God-sized capacity of strength and love, our actions and words will ring hollow in the midst of those who suffer around us. Steve Camp, one of my favorite Christian artists wrote a song, "Don't Tell Them Jesus Loves Them" that expresses it well:

> *Don't tell them Jesus loves them till you're ready to love them too;*
> *'Till your heart breaks from the sorrow and the pain they're going through. With a life full of compassion may we do what we must do. Don't tell them Jesus loves them till you're ready to love them too.*[9]

### OKAY, I'M IN—NOW, WHO AND WHAT DO I PRAY FOR?

Intercession requires information about those for whom we are praying. Where can we get the information we need to know what we can specifically pray for? I know at this point I'm going to sound like a broken record but the best place to start is the Bible:

What did Moses pray for in Exodus 33:18 and Numbers 14:19?


What did Hezekiah pray for in 2 Kings 19:19?


David cried out for one thing in Psalms 5:2, 17:1, 39:12, 61:1, 102:1. What is it?

Read Matthew 5:44 and Luke 6:28.
What do we do to those who persecute us?

Read what Jesus told His disciples to pray for in Luke 22:40.

Paul prayed for the Ephesian believers in Ephesians 1:18.
What did he pray for?

Look at 2 Thessalonians 1:11 What are the specific things that Paul prayed for on behalf of the believers in Thessalonica?

## COMMIT THE WORD OF GOD TO OUR HEARTS

*We must pray.* Secondly, we must not ignore the daily study, appreciation, and memorization of God's Word. Do you have a solid enough grasp of the truth of the Bible to explain why there is so much suffering around us? Can you use Scripture to show that God wants the church to be the agents of change for our suffering world? Can you give a clear presentation of the gospel using God's Word?

We need to study the Word, because we need to know what message we've been given to proclaim as ambassadors for Christ. We must be able to use the Bible effectively and efficiently to defend our beliefs and spur others to evangelistic and social action.

Imagine if an ambassador from the U.S. stood before the ruler of another country and was asked, "What message have you brought me from your president?" What if the ambassador responded, "The United States in the only nation that can assist you with your current crisis."

Then ruler then asked, "Why should I believe what you say? What do you have to show me to verify your claims of unique assistance?" What if the ambassador then said, "Well, I don't know exactly why my president is so confident. He's a very good man and I'm sure that he has reasons for saying that we're the *only* nation that can help you. I trust him because he's helped me when I had a family crisis."

That answer wouldn't be enough to move the foreign leader to believe in our president. To make a claim of exclusivity requires an adequate defense for such exclusivity. Peter said that we too, as Christ-followers, must

Right now, off the top of your head write down what you would tell someone who wanted to know how to become a Christian, using Scripture references if you can remember them. Was it harder than you thought?

Now write down the references of the passages you would share with someone who wanted to understand why you were serving them in their need.

"always be ready to give a defense to anyone who asks you for a reason for the hope that is in you" (1 Peter 3:15). We're ambassadors for Christ. As such, we need to know the message of Christ.

## DOERS

One of my favorite passages is Joshua 1:8. Having given him leadership of Israel, God instructed Joshua: "Don't let the book of the Law depart from your mouth." At the time, Joshua had the only five books of the Old Testament that had been written: Genesis, Exodus, Leviticus, Numbers, and Deuteronomy. These five books were what God was referring to when He told Joshua not to "let *the Book of the Law* depart from your mouth. Meditate on it day and night, so that you may be careful to do everything written in it."

Joshua's command from God was not just to know the Word. Joshua needed to know the Word of God for one singular purpose—in order to *do everything written in it.*

We must know the Word of God, but that knowledge is of little value if we fail to do what it says. James painted a very clear and very depressing picture of the man or woman who knows the Word of God but fails to live it out in his or her life:

"But be doers of the word and not hearers only, deceiving yourselves. Because if anyone is a hearer of the word and not a doer, he is like a man looking at his own face in a mirror; for he looks at himself, goes away, and right away forgets what kind of man he was. But the one who looks intently into the perfect law of freedom and perseveres in it, and is not a forgetful hearer but a doer who acts—this person will be blessed in what he does" (James 1:22-25).

We don't learn Scripture just to learn Scripture. To put it another way, we don't learn Scripture to pass a Scripture test. None of us become magnificent men or women of God by memorizing Scripture unless the memorization of the Scripture leads to action based on what we have learned.

Do you agree with that conclusion?
Why or why not?

Listen to "Heal This Land" by The Longing on your playlist.

Are you actively praying that God would bring His kingdom to reality?

There are a whole lot of people who know a lot of Bible but aren't out there *doing* anything. In essence, James said, "Hey, knowing the Word doesn't count for anything unless that knowledge results in godly activity." If we know Scripture yet we are not learning how to live it, we are deceiving ourselves. We look in the mirror and see ourselves as godly, but we aren't. A godly life is built on Scripture-informed action.

Paul emphasized this point in his letter to the Philippians: "Do what you have learned and received and heard and seen in me, and the God of peace will be with you" (Philippians 4:9). He had in mind that the things we've learned from God would lead us to success in our acts of ministry, service, and sacrifice. Through the daily study and ingestion of the Word of God we can learn to see this world from God's perspective and translate that perspective into concrete and practical action.

My passion for this topic of poverty, injustice, suffering, and God's heart for the poor came by reading Scripture. The Word of God transformed me as I read, reflected, memorized, and then acted upon God's truth. I began to see people through God's eyes as He revealed both His heart and the true condition of our world. I have not "arrived" by any stretch of the imagination; I preached for ten years before the two-edged sword of the Bible pierced my heart. My transformation came from the Spirit of God transforming me through the Word of God.

## SPEAK

I realize that prayer and Bible study are fairly straightforward disciplines that can be privately practiced and incorporated into our lifestyle in isolation. Speaking out about these issues is another matter. For some, the idea of speaking out about poverty and injustice feels a lot like joining a picket line. Like that avenue of protest, speaking about social issues might feel distinctly political to you, and anything political is bound to be controversial.

Many believers are uncomfortable speaking about anything that might prompt disagreement from others. Nevertheless, we simply must create awareness of the plight of our world by speaking about these issues in our daily conversations. We can bring about change by the use of our words as well as our actions. Christians have often used the spoken word, dialogue, and debate as the catalysts for lasting change. Opening dialogue on these issues can lead to mutual encouragement, education, awareness, transformation in the hearts and minds of others, and increased conviction of our need to be involved.

The most effective way to start the process of dialogue about these issues is to begin the conversation within our own sphere of influence. When we're at lunch with our friends or in our small group we can create conversation around the latest development (large or small) that has hit the news channels. We can challenge each other by asking, "What has God called us to do, say, or pray concerning this situation?" In doing so, we can take our relationships to the next level. Through our community, we can begin to actually impact the world rather than just watch movies and go to concerts together.

> What are the difficulties in speaking out about politically charged issues?

> How should that influence our speech about such issues?

> What would keep you from beginning the conversation of social change with those in your community?

Paul told the church at Corinth to give generously and preach the gospel. These are the two things that we've been talking about through this study—giving sacrificially and preaching the gospel. Then Paul went on to describe the result of the Corinthians' words and deeds: "Through the proof of this service, *they will glorify God for your obedience to the confession of the gospel of Christ, and for your generosity in sharing with them and with others*" (2 Corinthians 9:13, *emphasis added*). According to Paul, people will praise the name of God because the Corinthians were willing to speak of Christ and act on His behalf. The end result of our words and works becomes visible when people see those good deeds and hear the message of hope in Jesus . . . and praise God. We work, we speak, we pray, and we go so that ultimately, God might receive the glory that He deserves.

## CHANGE

One of the most difficult things that we experience in life is change. Change, regardless of its magnitude, is usually accompanied by stress and uncertainty. Recently, I was talking to a friend about why it is so difficult for real change to occur in our lives. In a burst of frustration, I said something like, "You know, it's hard to move people from one place to another, even if it's exactly where God wants them to go." He responded, "Well, you've got to understand, Todd—change is a process."

Change comes, first of all, with information. The information we have about God's heart for the poor is not new information, but it is neglected information. We need to help each other understand the issues we are confronting by re-discovering everything the Lord has for us in Scripture.

After that re-discovery, God will begin to move inside us to develop a new attitude that is in line with His character and purposes. I see this time and time again in the lives of people. A little information makes a world of difference in God's hands. He can take the smallest of suggestions and change someone's entire worldview.

Information leads to attitude change, and attitude change leads to conviction. Conviction causes our choices to change in response to the truth we've learned. Paul described this process well in Romans 12:2: "Do not be conformed to this age, but be transformed by the renewing of your mind, so that you may discern what is the good, pleasing, and perfect will of God."

We are renewed by saturating our minds with the Word of God.

Another friend of mine, David Edwards, explained it this way: "A thought left in your mind long enough develops into a belief; and it is beliefs that dictate our actions." My hope is that our meditation upon the scriptural truths we've studied so far have renewed our minds by becoming deep seeded beliefs. Those beliefs will begin to dictate our actions from this day on in relation to our role in changing the world through word and deed.

Eventually we—as changed individuals—can come together as those with renewed passion for justice and compassion and enact real corporate change. Rediscovered information, new attitude and conviction, change of actions on a personal level, and then change of actions on a corporate level—these four components are used by God so that collectively our passions can fuse to truly change the world.

# CHANGE

It's time for an honest examination of lifestyle. This week, keep a record of every, single expenditure, from soda to car insurance. At the end of the week, break down the expenditures into large categories like transportation, food, and entertainment. I think you'll be intrigued at the results . . .

After you have your results, **ask yourself this question**: What can I cut down or remove from my life to free up excess income to help others?

Make some tough decisions. Resolve to drink less coffee, see fewer movies, or use less power. Then pick a program of your choice—preferably one associated with the church (ask your group leader for a list of suggestions)—that is active in the realm of social justice. Start giving away what you saved.

NAME: **JEREMY AND JAMIE PHILLIPS**

JOB OR MINISTRY: **EMPOWER AFRICAN CHILDREN, UGANDA, AFRICA**

**WWW.EMPOWERAFRICANCHILDREN.ORG**

# THE WAY OF THE HEART

What breaks your heart? For Jeremy and Jamie Phillips, it's Africa. "If something is on your heart and something hurts you inside and you don't feel right doing anything else, then you've got to do it," Jamie says.

For most of their lives, both have been drawn to ministry and the opportunity to help other people. "I had grown up with everything handed to me and felt like I wanted to do something useful with my life," Jamie expresses.

After volunteering separately in different parts of Africa, Jeremy and Jamie got married in 1999. They tried living in Colorado for a short time but knew that God wanted them in Africa. Soon an opportunity arose to work with children in Uganda through an organization called Uganda Children's Charity Function (UCCF). So the newlyweds packed a few possessions, said good-bye to their family and friends, and moved to the other side of the world.

Once settled in the rural southwest part of Uganda, the Phillips' realized that ministering to the village there would be challenging. "One of the things we wanted to do was be in Uganda and not feel like visitors," Jamie explains. "[But] when you're white, you really stand out; and everybody knows you're different. We just wanted to be with [the villagers] as much as possible and figure out what their lives were like."

The language barrier made it difficult for them to develop deep relationships with the people, and they experienced a great deal of loneliness. Although they went expecting to help with land development, they ended up being in leadership. Jamie served as a matron and Jeremy as the headmaster for an orphanage where they worked with more than 200 orphans, most affected by AIDS.

When their work ended and the Phillips moved back to Colorado, they had their first child and loved being surrounded by family. "We're from Colorado, and we love it. Our families are there. We had just bought our first house, and it was so cute. We had a healthy baby. Jeremy's job was going well, and I had a good job. And life was great. I said to Jeremy that something was a little too easy; it just felt like God was going to do something," Jamie says.

When Jeremy was asked to start a new ministry, Empower African Children, they knew God wanted them to reconnect with their passion. Once again, the Phillips' family, with a new baby on the way, packed up and moved—this time to Dallas, where the organization is currently headquartered. But it would not surprise them if they eventually moved back to Uganda.

Empower African Children is an organization that provides relief to AIDS orphans and children who are kidnapped and forced to be soldiers. It also embraces and celebrates the artistic abilities of African children. The children's troupe shares African culture with people in the United States through singing, dancing, and drama. The organization hopes to expand to include other art forms such as painting and drawing.

"The tour is for the kids in a sense that they are developing amazing artistic skills. They are like professional singers and dancers. It would blow your mind. It helps people sense what art does for a child. It also raises awareness over here," Jamie says.

A quote by Bob Pierce, the founder of World Vision, "Let my heart be broken by the things that break the heart of God," really resonates with Jeremy and Jamie. "Our longing and the passion in our hearts has always been for the AIDS orphans in Africa," Jamie says. "Our hearts are broken by the children, and there's nothing else that we can do with our lives—it would seem meaningless to us."

---

## "LET MY HEART BE BROKEN BY THE THINGS THAT BREAK THE HEART OF GOD,"
— BOB PIERCE, FOUNDER OF WORLD VISION

# LETTING THE RUBBER MEET THE ROAD

The word *need* gets thrown around far too often in Western society today. Our idea of what we need has moved far beyond the realm of food, water, clothing, shelter, and companionship. Now we need cable television. We need designer clothes. We need expensive coffee and coffee-like drinks. We need a cell phone and we need a wireless router. I wonder if what we really *need* is to stop *needing* so much.

The world will not be changed until God's people are willing to actually make some changes in their lifestyle to embrace God's heart for the poor. That means real, tangible sacrifice of those things we have mistaken for needs. It means being willing to give up time, money, energy, and comfort for the sake of others. Until we are willing to give in a way that hurts us a little bit, we will miss out on the chance God is giving us to play an active role in changing the world. I don't know about you, but I *need* that opportunity.

## WHAT DO YOU NEED?

Give, and it will be given to you; a good measure—pressed down, shaken together, and running over—will be poured into your lap. For with the measure you use, it will be measured back to you.

LUKE 6:38

# LETTING THE RUBBER MEET THE ROAD

### EXAMINATION

Several months ago, nearly two hundred of our young adults participated in "Examined Lifestyle Month." Each participant received a devotional book written by members of our International Poverty and Justice Ministry (the educational arm of our Global Missions division). The goal was simple: spend a month reflecting on biblical commands about possessions, generosity, and the poor. Each young adult was instructed to read the daily devotionals that related to those subjects. Additionally, they were asked to consider what they would have to give up in order to live at the U.S. poverty line of $9,800 per person per year. At the end of the month, they were asked to identify at least three regular expenditures that are not necessities. They were challenged to give up these items and give the savings to the church or other Christian organizations that served people in the greatest need. Although one of the goals was to help people in need, the primary goal was to learn about the true meaning and impact of generosity.

**Read the following verses:**

MARK 10:17-22
MATTHEW 25:31-40
LUKE 6:30
LUKE 12:33-34
JAMES 2:15-16

Write down what comes to mind as you read each of these passages.

Some decided to give up cable television, decrease spending on clothes by a certain amount, or stop going to Starbucks. One young woman took her savings and sponsored five children through World Vision. Others decided that they would purchase a less expensive car and give the money they saved to our missions division as scholarships for short-term mission trips. The stories are many but the results were the same: those who participated were molded, shaped, and matured by the Spirit of God through their acts of reflection and generosity. We were created by God to give—to give of our possessions, our time, our talents, and ourselves.

One of the greatest treatises on giving and generosity was penned by Paul under the direction of the Holy Spirit to the church at Corinth:

"Remember this: the person who sows sparingly will also reap sparingly, and the person who sows generously will also reap generously. Each person should do as he has decided in his heart—not out of regret or out of necessity, for God loves a cheerful giver. And God is able to make every grace overflow to you, so that in every way, always having everything you need, you may excel in every good work. As it is written:

"He has scattered; He has given to the poor;
His righteousness endures forever."

Now the One who provides seed for the sower and bread for food will provide and multiply your seed and increase the harvest of your righteousness, as you are enriched in every way for all generosity, which produces thanksgiving to God through us. For the ministry of this service is not only supplying the needs of the saints, but is also overflowing in many acts of thanksgiving to God.

Through the proof of this service, they will glorify God for your obedience to the confession of the gospel of Christ, and for your generosity in sharing with them and with others. And in their prayers for you they will have deep affection for you because of the surpassing grace of God on you. Thanks be to God for His indescribable gift" (2 Corinthians 9:6-15).

## GIVE

We can *pray*—intercede for others in their need. We can *study*—inscribe the Word of God on our hearts in relation to the 2,000 verses addressing the issues of poverty, injustice, oppression, hunger, illness, and disease. We can *speak*—telling others of what we have learned and challenging them to join us in changing the world for maybe one last time. We can also *give*. Here's where the rubber meets the road. We all have some- . thing that we can give to meet the needs of others. We can give money, time, talent, prayer, and our words of insight.

When we give we experience one of the most perplexing ironies of Scripture: "Give, and it will be given to you . . . " (Luke 6:38). That statement alone is powerful enough in its implications for our lives as Christ-followers. But Jesus didn't stop there; He continued by describing the abundance of what we receive when we give. He described what we'll receive as " . . . a good measure—pressed down, shaken together, and running over—will be poured into your lap." Now that's abundance! Then the Son of God said, "For with the measure you use, it will be measured back to you."

Are you being selfish if you give and get something in return?

Why is it that we hold so tightly to our possessions?

Listen to "Fair Trade" before your group gets together to discuss this session. (Your group leader will send it to you via email.) How can you be more socially aware in your daily actions?

This passage reveals the glaring irony of our sinful condition. The world says "take all you can get" while God shouts "give all you've got!" It should be clear that you can't do both. We're meant to be givers but some of us have only lived life as *takers*. Consider this: In His statement in Luke 6:38, Jesus was trying to convince people to give of themselves. That means that Jesus actually has to talk us into *receiving* abundantly. Have you ever *really* thought about that? Why would any of us have to be talked into that? Yet we cling tightly to everything we think belongs to us. Let me illustrate.

Take your hands and squeeze them together right now as tightly as you can. Hold them, if you can, until I tell you to stop, OK? It won't be too long, just hold them real tight. Really squeeze; really press them together. You know what? That's exactly what some of us, if not many of us, are doing in our lives. We do this with our money, relationships, and jobs. We wonder why we are a stressed out culture; it's because we're holding tightly to anything and everything we can get our hands on.

DON'T LOOSEN THOSE HANDS. Keep holding them tightly. What I want you to do now while you're holding really tightly is . . . just let go. Release your grip and completely relax your hands. Notice how the life-giving blood rushes back to your palms and fingers. Sense the change that comes in your breathing and heart rate as you loosen your grip. Consider the difference in your attitude as you stop holding on.

There is an axiomatic law in the universe: the more you give, the more you get back. Let me say that again: *the more you give, the more you get back*. Jesus tried to tell us this so many times. He used stories and illustrations. His very life is about giving, pouring Himself out, expecting nothing in return because He knows that God the Father will pour into Him good measure, pressed down, shaken together, running over. He knows and lives this truth. The more He gives, the more He receives. That's a truth in our life as well.

### HEALTH AND WEALTH?

Unfortunately, this whole concept has been misused and abused in churches that preach a "health and wealth gospel" or what some call the "prosperity gospel." The idea behind the "prosperity gospel" (a uniquely American distortion of the Bible) is that God wants His people to be wealthy, in perfect health, and free from trial in life. One only needs to read a little bit of the Bible to begin to ask the obvious questions: "If we are all supposed to be wealthy, then why wasn't Jesus the wealthiest person in Israel? If we are meant to be trouble free, then why does James speak of the troubles to come and say they have a redemptive purpose in our lives? If we are all supposed to be perfectly healthy, then why was Job, a righteous man, allowed to be stricken with sickness?"

The idea is ludicrous. Despite these misinterpretations and irresponsible use of Scripture, the truth of Jesus' promise about giving and receiving remains powerful. For example, the more we pour out our relationships, the more we receive. It's a universal truth, right? The more I pour time and love and attention into my children, the more I receive from those relationships. Unfortunately, the less we pour into relationships with family and friends the less we get back. This universal truth works both ways.

What about our jobs? The more we pour out, the more we receive. I used to be in sales at Dell Inc. I was a 6-month-old believer when I started working there. I realized I had a unique opportunity to test the Word of God at this new job. I could try to take all I could by saying whatever I had to say to make the sale and help myself and no one else. Or, I could test this newly found universal truth of giving and receiving. Instead of bending the truth for a sale, I was honest with my customers about what they needed for their computer systems, being careful never to sell them something more than they needed. I was honest about shipping times even if it cost me the sale. I also forced myself to help new employees and offered to help my fellow employees close sales on their days off asking for nothing in return.

Did I make a fortune for my decision to give? Did I get promoted? I did make my quota each month, and I was eventually promoted from personal sales to small business sales, but so were a lot of employees who chose to "look out for number one." So what did I receive for what I gave? I received unspeakable joy as those formerly new employees chose to follow my lead and help the new employees who came behind them. I got the satisfaction of having customers send their friends to me to help them with their computer purchase.

But the real return came as other employees saw the way I chose to live my professional life and began asking more about my faith in Jesus. God gave me the opportunity to share my faith with literally dozens of fellow workers, several of whom became brothers and sisters in Christ. I gave, and God gave back to me in "good measure—pressed down, shaken together, and running over." When we do all we do for the Lord we will

The film "In America" is an interesting commentary on true generosity and help. Grab a friend and take a look at this thought-provoking movie.

receive in good measure, and God's choice of blessing takes many wonderful forms.

Scripture says that if you will simply pour yourself out, expecting nothing in return from the world, God will pour into you. Does that mean that if you give a hundred you get a thousand back? No, it's not an equation thing.

Jesus said, "For with the measure you use, it will be measured back to you." In other words, if you pour out of yourself for His sake, He will pour into you for His sake. God promises that He will make us mature and complete, not lacking anything if we pursue Him in trials, pour out to others, and seek His Kingdom first. Joy is our reward. Maturity is our reward. He is our reward! And, yes, sometimes God rewards us with material things, but those rewards pale in comparison to the gifts of character and maturity we receive.

> Think about some of the ways you have blessed others
> with your time, talents, money, or prayer.
>
> When you gave, what, if anything, did you receive?
> (joy, maturity, wisdom, material blessings)

As I've gone through this process of re-education regarding these social issues, one of the things that my wife and I prayerfully decided to do was to sponsor a child in a third-world country for each of our kids. So we have sponsored three children who are the same sex and exactly the same age as each of our children. Eric has the same birthday and is the same age as our son, Parker. Parker is able to send Eric letters, small gifts, and tell him about Jesus. Parker prays for Eric at night before he goes to bed. Parker is going to grow up with him and always think of Eric on his birthday. This is a small but significant start for our children. They will grow up pouring out to others, expecting nothing in return from them. They will only experience God filling them up to overflowing with joy and maturity through their acts of giving.

## TOUCH
Pray, study, speak, give . . . but nothing takes the place of touch. By 'touch,' I mean direct involvement. We must get actively involved in the lives of others in need. The Book of Matthew provides some profound examples of Jesus' ministry of touch:

84

"Reaching our His hand He *touched* him, saying, 'I am willing; be made clean'" (Matthew 8:3a, *emphasis added*).

"So He *touched* her hand, and the fever left her" (Matthew 8:15a, *emphasis added*).

"Then He t*ouched* their eyes . . . and their eyes were opened" (Matthew 9:29-30a, *emphasis added*).

"They . . . brought to Him all who were sick. They were begging Him that they might only *touch* the tassel on His robe. And as many as *touched* it were made perfectly well" (Matthew 14:35-36, *emphasis added*).

Jesus' ministry of touch is amazing to me. Jesus was willing to break social and religious norms. He met the physical needs of people as He taught in towns and villages. He did exactly what we have talked about: good works as He proclaimed the kingdom. In that preaching and doing, Jesus physically extended the hand of God to touch those in need.

> Read Luke 9:1-2.
> What did Jesus ask His followers to do with the power and authority He gave them?

God intensely desires for everybody who professes faith in Jesus Christ to be directly involved in ministry to others in such a way that believers are close enough to touch the hurting where they are.

If you are one of the many followers of Christ who have yet to go on a short-term mission trip; if you have yet to get actively involved in a local ministry in which you have direct contact with those in need; if you have never "smelled" and "tasted" real poverty, then you are missing a huge part of the experience of being a follower of Christ.

Until you have come close enough to those who are truly suffering to hug them, speak words of encouragement to them, to *touch* them, you have not experienced all of what God offers His followers. God wants us all to follow Him by developing our own ministry of touch.

In every city on our globe, you can get involved in ministering to the poor and needy. God wants you to start in the town that you call home, but your involvement doesn't end there. My prayer is that everyone who works through this study will eventually set foot on foreign soil, prefera-bly third-world foreign soil, on a short-term mission trip so God can give each one of you a perspective on what He's doing around this world.

Watch "Daybreak: An Experiment in Truth" when your group meets. Is there any passion in your life that God is pushing you towards for the sake of others?

How does it make you feel to know that I'm praying for you to actually go on a short-term mission trip to a third-world country?

Does it excite you, or does the prospect of going on even a short-term mission trip anywhere give you pause?

For a great example of the ministry of touch, read the inspiring book written by Mother Theresa, *In My Own Words*.

## A TREND THAT MUST BE REVERSED

There is a disturbing phenomenon happening in American churches today. We are outsourcing our ministries of touch to other organizations. We let Campus Crusade touch the lives of college students. We let World Vision touch the lives of children in third-world countries. We let Meals-On-Wheels touch the lives of the sick and elderly. We let Goodwill touch the lives of people in need of clothing. We let Habitat for Humanity touch the lives of countless families who need shelter.

All of these organizations are wonderful and are doing good things. But instead of embracing its role as the agent of change for the world, the church is quietly abdicating its world-changing mission to these groups. We outsource our ministry of compassion and touch. We separate ourselves from intimate contact with the needy. We have suburbanized our churches and created consumer-minded congregations.

What are some other examples you see of churches outsourcing their ministry of touch?

How does this happen in your own church?

The decision may be subconscious, but we are outsourcing our compassion. Many in church prefer programs that focus on their perceived needs and the perceived needs of their kids. No one would say, "I don't want to go on a mission trip," but many will argue, "I'm not comfortable outside the United States. But I'd be glad to write a check for someone else to go do that crazy stuff." I talk to countless people who write checks, basically paying others to serve on behalf of the body. Someone will tell me, "I support several missionaries." "Ever been on a trip yourself?" "No, are you kidding? I don't know a foreign language and it's just plain dangerous outside the U.S."

I can't even begin to address the myriad of problems associated with this kind of thinking, but the biggest one is that it's flat-out unbiblical. Giving is good. Giving is necessary. But when we allow giving to absolutely replace a first-hand ministry of touch, we rob ourselves of the experience of caring for others as Jesus did as well as limit the number of those in need that receive the physical touch of the representatives of Christ.

> Do you think the scenario above is an accurate representation of many people in churches today? Why or Why not?

> Do you think it describes your perspective on mission activity and missionaries up to this point?

We are all challenged to wrestle with the part we're to play in the Great Commission: "mak[ing] disciples of all nations, baptizing them in the name of the Father and of the Son and of the Holy Spirit, teaching them to observe everything I have commanded you" (Matthew 28:19-20a).

I've been at churches where the missionaries are corporately supported. The church may have thousands of members and there are only three or four missionaries who know another language and have committed to long-term international service. The rest of the church writes checks to support "their missionaries" as though these people are somehow different than the rest of the members in the church. While they may have a unique invitation from God to serve permanently in a foreign country, but they are not unique in their obedience to the scope of the Great Commission to make disciples of all nations. We're all supposed to be out there; not necessarily to be career missionaries, but we are all called to wrestle with our involvement in the global mission of God.

The only way we can truly do that is by going out and by being personally involved in a ministry of touch where there is need.

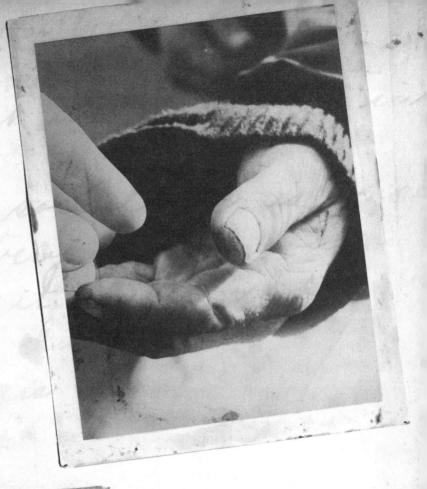

## TOUCH

Now get ready to go. There is a time to send and a time to go. Everyone needs to go at some point. What would it take for you to be on a short-term mission trip with a church in your area? What would you have to sacrifice? What would you have to change? Is it worth it?

Without intentionality, you will neglect your ministry of touch. So let's be intentional—find a church in your area that is planning a mission experience and sign up. Fight through the logical objections. Battle past your hesitations. Take a chance and sign up.

In the meantime, be intentional about finding ways you can directly touch others. Seek out an assisted living facility, a homeless ministry, or a children's home—somewhere you can be with the people you are serving. Then go; serve; touch.

NAME: **JULIA HARPER**

JOB OR MINISTRY: **DAYBREAK MINISTRIES, WASHINGTON D.C.**

# BREAKING THROUGH

DayBreak—an after school program and Saturday outreach ministry—began as all good things begin. A few people saw a need that God had been preparing their hearts to meet. One of those few was Julia Harper.

In 2000, a group of people held a carnival as an outreach to the children of their community. Julia Harper was among those who had been praying and looking for a way they could minister to kids in one of the neediest communities in the city. "God was exposing me to the people he was grooming me to serve—he was preparing my heart to serve."

In the midst of a season in which Julia felt as if God was calling her to focus—stop and listen to His voice—DayBreak happened. "I wanted to serve. I thought I'd be a teacher; I never in my wildest dreams thought DayBreak would be the means God used for me to serve," she says.

What exists today, in the form of DayBreak Ministries, is a program for inner-city kids—specifically children who live in Lincoln Heights— that offers after school programming, tutoring, and Bible studies. DayBreak is designed to give neighborhood kids a place to play, study, and have a meal.

While it is a staffed organization, volunteers make the work happen. Most of the volunteers who serve with DayBreak are single 20- or 30-somethings who have the time and ability to use resources at this stage in life. "God has ordained our volunteers to be here and He then makes sure that they have all they need," Julia says. "They've been used powerfully, not because they look like they fit the part, but because God has a plan for them to be here. "

As for fears, Julia is at ease in what some would view as a dangerous environment: "I'm called to be here. God has hemmed me in on every side. If something happens to me then I know that God's hand is on me and He's allowed that to happen because He's going to further ministry through it."

She reflects on what has become of the stirrings in her heart: "I had no idea what this was going to turn into." She listened to the Lord and acted on it—the rest is history.

TO SEE WHAT TAKES PLACE AT DAYBREAK, WATCH THE DOCUMENTARY THAT ACCOMPANIES THIS STUDY FOUND IN THE GET UNCOMFORTABLE LEADER KIT. YOU'LL ALSO FIND AN EXTENDED INTERVIEW WITH JULIA ABOUT HER EXPERIENCES SERVING HER COMMUNITY.

# CHANGING THE WORLD IN GOD'S STRENGTH

Call me an idealist if you want to. After all, changing the world is an awfully tall order, especially for people like us. How can we change the world? We have trouble keeping our own lives in order, much less being an integral part of social change.

Here's the bad news: you're right. We can't change the world. At best, we can drum up some local support and maybe talk ourselves into caring for a while about stuff we didn't used to concern ourselves with. But consider this: changing the world really that tall of an order for God? Let's keep in mind that He's done it before.

He has used stuttering leaders, lusty kings, pouting prophets, prideful teenagers, uneducated fishermen, and self-righteous know-it-alls. The common characteristic of all of these world-changers was not their education, income level, stability, or charisma—it was their availability. They were available for the task, and God used His power to change the world through them.

If anyone speaks, his speech should be like the oracles of God; if anyone serves, his service should be from the strength God provides, so that in everything God may be glorified through Jesus Christ. To Him belong the glory and the power forever and ever. Amen.

1 PETER 4:11

# CHANGING THE WORLD IN GOD'S STRENGTH

## AVAILABILITY

This final chapter should be extremely encouraging for those of us who still find it hard to imagine getting intimately involved with the suffering and oppression throughout the world. Be certain of this—God does not give His children any assignment that He will not empower them to accomplish. To put it another way, God will not give us a task without empowering us by His Spirit to bring it to fruition.

That truth is essential to our understanding of everything that we've talked about in relation to God's mission to provide for those in greatest need and offer His Son to all. Hebrews 13:20-21 says, "Now may the God of peace . . . equip you with all that is good to do His will, working in us what is pleasing in His sight, through Jesus Christ, to whom be glory forever and ever." God can and will equip us to do everything that He has called us to do.

Ultimately God will accomplish what He wills to accomplish. He chooses those who are available to be used by Him to accomplish His tasks and gives them power and perseverance through His Spirit to be His chosen vessels. Availability—not power, position, expertise, or wealth—has always been a quality that God has looked for in His followers. From Abraham to Moses, from the prophet Isaiah to Paul, God has chosen men and women for no other perceivable reason than their availability.

The question then for each of us is this: Are we going to make ourselves available to God? Are we going to allow our faith to increase so that He might empower us to be actively involved in His redemptive plan for mankind? The word *empower* simply means to equip or supply with an ability. So when I say there is nothing we can do apart from the empowerment of the Holy Spirit, I mean that God's Spirit literally gives us the very ability to do the works that He has called us to do. The ability to pour out our time, energy, prayer, and resources all comes from the Spirit of God.

Jesus was crucified, buried, resurrected, and ministered for 40 days among His followers. Hundreds and hundreds of people saw Him in His glorified body (1 Corinthians 15:3-6). In this miraculous series of events He defeated the power and penalty of sin and the sting of death for all of us who believe in Him.

Having accomplished those things, Jesus stood before His disciples and said to them, "But you will receive power when the Holy Spirit has come upon you, and you will be My witnesses in Jerusalem, and all Judea and Samaria, and to the ends of the earth" (Acts 1:8). Jesus told His followers that the Holy Spirit would in every way empower them to be God's witness to the gospel message of His love, mercy and justice in.

I Corinthians 2:14 says, "But the natural man does not welcome what comes from God's Spirit, because it is foolishness to him; he is not able to know it since it is evaluated spiritually." Paul was explaining to the believers in Corinth that without the Spirit of God in them, they simply could not understand the things that come from God. But for those who have the Spirit of God living in them, the pages of the Bible come to life like a child's pop-up book. The Spirit guides us into all truth (John 16:13) and then empowers us to do the will of God.

## EMPOWERING THE AVAILABLE

It is in the strength of the Spirit of God—not in our own strength—that we are able to do anything that God invites us to do. He promises His power in Acts 1:8, so that we are able to be His witnesses to the awesome treasure we found in having a relationship with the Father through the Son, Jesus Christ. The first thing we can count on then is God's willingness to pour Himself out to the world through us. He uses our willingness, faith, and availability to pour His love out through us to a lost and hopeless world. He accomplishes this through His Spirit, whom He gave us. What an awesome gift.

Empowerment is the responsibility of the Holy Spirit of God who lives in all followers of Christ. When we believe in Jesus Christ as our Lord and Savior, God the Father sends His Spirit to live in us to mark us as believers (Ephesians 4:30), guide us into all truth, comfort us, and empower us to do the impossible. Remember, "What is impossible with men is possible with God" (Luke 18:27).

What is the difference between serving in your strength and being empowered by the Holy Spirit?

How can you be sure you are not serving in your own strength?

Read the following verses about the Holy Spirit working in our lives and write down the key point of each verse:

1 CORINTHIANS 2:14
LUKE 11:13
LUKE 12:1
JOHN 14:26
JOHN 16:13
ROMANS 14:17
ROMANS 15:13
EPHESIANS 4:30
1 THESSALONIANS 1:6
2 TIMOTHY 1:14

There are many things the Spirit does, but one of His main functions is to empower the children of God to be His agents of change in the world through the proclamation of the gospel and good works. The main way we're empowered to do these good works is through spiritual gifts.

As a Christ-follower, you have been given at least one spiritual gift straight out of heaven into your life for the purposes of proclaiming the gospel and doing good works so that His kingdom might be increased in this world as it is in heaven.

Look up 1 Peter 4:10-11.
Who are we called to serve?


Why are we called to serve them?


Listen to "Sustaining Me" by Spur58 on your playlist. What do you think it would be like to live totally dependent on God?

Whatever gift you've received from God, you're to use that gift to serve others, "faithfully administering God's grace in its various forms" so that God may be praised. In 1 Peter 4:11, Peter placed spiritual gifts into two categories: *speech* and *service*. He wrote, "If anyone *speaks,* his speech should be like the oracles of God" *(emphasis added)*. We talked earlier about being an *ambassador* for Christ and speaking the words of God as though He was there (2 Corinthians 5:18-20). That's exactly what we're doing with these gifts. Remember, you don't need to get creative about the message. We just speak the truth of the gospel; that's what we're called to do.

First Peter 4:11 continues, "If anyone *serves,* his service should be from the strength God provides . . . " *(emphasis added)*. We are to do the things that God has called us to do in His strength rather than our own. In other words, strength is going to come from God to do the things He's called us to do in the first place. The reason for this is made clear at the end of verse 11: " . . . so that in everything, *God may be glorified through Jesus Christ.* To Him belong the glory and the power forever and ever. Amen" *(emphasis added)*.

The purpose of proclaiming the gospel and the purpose of doing the good works is so that in all things God may be praised through Jesus Christ. All of our words and all of our service is to be done in the strength provided by the Spirit of God so that those we serve might come to know Jesus and glorify our Father in Heaven.

Think back to a time when you served in your own strength. What are some things that happen when you serve in your own strength?

How did that experience affect your attitude about service in general?

We may each have one gift, or two, or ten. Some of us have been given many of the various gifts that are described in different passages of the Bible. It doesn't matter, though, whether you've got one, two, or ten. It doesn't make you any greater or any lesser than anyone else. The number of gifts is not important. God has a specific plan for the gifts He's given each of us for the time in which we live. We're supposed to use whatever gifts we have received for God's purposes in the world.

Our ability to accomplish the things of God has nothing to do with our own human ability. We simply cannot sustain a life of service and sacrifice in our own power. If we try—and I know that some of us have—we will eventually become jaded, angry, and numb. Every godly work requires God's power. You can go out and try really hard to help somebody, but the things we do that have the greatest effect happen only when we understand what God wants us to do and then allow God to do it through us under His power. If we try to do it on our own we'll run out of steam.

Our lives are to be poured out indiscriminately to others around us, expecting absolutely nothing in return. Sounds pretty selfless . . . and it is. The problem is none of us are capable of doing this; it's impossible. But God can and will live this kind of selfless life through us in His endless power. If we let God work through us to live these radically selfless lives, then we become like a stream of living water, channeling God's love to those in need.

Most of the time, though, we feel more like dried up wells than streams of living water. Interestingly enough, we are usually very busy doing good things during the dry times. Despite the amount of activities we are participating in we feel completely spent and don't experience the

"filling up" that God promises. Perhaps we are dry because we are doing a lot of good things but not doing the *one* "God-thing" we've been called by God to do. Consider this: *God only empowers us to do the things He's called us to do.*

A lot of Christ-followers are feverishly serving in many areas but seeing few results. Maybe God is trying to get the attention of these believers and ask them, "Did I ask you to sponsor five kids, sign up for three mission trips in six months, help out three nights a week at the soup kitchen, and lead your Bible study group? No! I invited you to do one thing—prayerfully prepare for one mission trip. That's it. I have other people in mind for the other activities and frankly, you're in the way of *their* opportunity to serve." We can get so caught up in doing good things that we fail to actually spend the bulk of who we are on the *God things*—the stuff He actually invited us to do in His power.

What's worse, these other things that we do (that are good things but outside of God's plan for us at that moment) lessen our effectiveness in the activities God wants to do in and through us. When we choose to focus only on the things that God has called us to do, we find ourselves energized, empowered, and filled with passion. We are filled up to the point where we are overflowing with the heart of God. He pours into us to such a degree that His love and grace are spilling out onto those to whom He's called us to serve.

> If you are serving in some way right now, do you feel burned out or empowered and encouraged?

> Think about the reasons why or why not.

### SPIRIT-FILLED

The Bible refers to the Spirit of God as "the wind of God." As the divine wind, He blows at His pleasure; He goes where He pleases. A leaf that finds itself caught in the wind has no choice but to go wherever it is blown; the only option for an inanimate object caught in the breeze is to submit to the power of the wind. We, on the other hand, do have a choice. We can submit to the leading and power of something we cannot see.

Like the wind, the Holy Spirit is invisible; we can't see Him. We can only experience the result of the Spirit's activity in our lives and in the lives of the people we serve. We never know just where the Spirit will lead us and exactly what He'll invite us to do. When we submit to His leading—to the push of the wind—life really becomes an adventure. When we finally choose to truly surrender our lifestyles to God's plan for us life gets really good.

If we choose to submit to His leading, we will find ourselves in the amazing position of serving inside of the inexhaustible supply of God's strength. I find this to be true of myself as I stand to teach the Word of God.

God empowers me to teach the Bible. He has gifted me to do so, and He continues to supply the strength for the task. If He didn't empower me to do this, the well would have run dry about three days into my teaching career. But here I am, more than a decade later, and God continues to allow me to be part of His redemptive plan through teaching His Word and proclaiming the gospel while serving and sacrificing for those in need. When I preach and teach, I'm empowered. I'm filled up to overflowing. I get frustrated that I only have 30 minutes to preach each Sunday; I could go on and on because it's not my strength that is being expended. Rather, God consistently empowers me by His Spirit to proclaim His truth with passion and conviction.

He offers this same empowerment to each of us according to His unique plan for our lives. Preaching isn't any more important than any other spiritual gift or act of service done in the name of Jesus. God will do in you what He has done in me. He will make you so passionate about how and where you are serving that you will live your life desiring more opportunities to use your gifts in His service.

God wants to put His strength in those believers willing to do specifically what He invites them to do. Every time He pours out His power on someone, He does so for a purpose. As seen in Acts 1:8, God poured His Spirit out on the early church so that they would be His witnesses. Likewise, we are to be His witnesses by proclaiming the gospel and doing good works. The mission has not changed. We are simply the next in a long line of

Listen to "She Went" before your group gets together to discuss this session. (Your group leader will send it to you via email.) Consider where and when the Lord wants you to go.

generations who continue to proclaim the Gospel and do good works so that people might come to know Jesus and God's name might be glorified in all nations.

## AN INVITATION FOR INVOLVEMENT

There is an event recorded in Matthew that perfectly illustrates much of what we've been learning over the past six sessions:

**When evening came, the disciples approached Him and said, "This place is a wilderness, and it is already late. Send the crowds away so they can go into the villages and buy food for themselves."**

**"They don't need to go away," Jesus told them.
"You give them something to eat."**

**"But we only have five loaves and two fish here," they said to Him.**

**"Bring them here to Me," He said. Then He commanded the crowds to sit down on the grass. He took the five loaves and the two fish, and looking up to heaven, He blessed them. He broke the loaves and** *gave them to the disciples, and the disciples [gave them] to the crowds.* **Everyone ate and was filled. Then they picked up 12 baskets full of leftover pieces! Now those who ate were about 5,000 men, besides women and children (Matthew 14:15-21,** *emphasis added***).**

Jesus and His disciples were surrounded by 5,000 men, but likely there were many more if the women and children were included. At some point, the disciples realized that these thousands of onlookers were far from their villages and had nothing to eat. The disciples suggested to Jesus that He send them back to their villages to buy themselves dinner. Their first response was to let the masses fend for themselves.

Jesus had a different plan in mind. He suggested instead that the *disciples themselves* give the people something to eat. What could Jesus possibly have been thinking? How could these 12 disciples feed such a large number of people? Despite the impossibility of the task, Jesus sent them into the crowd to find whatever food was available. They returned with only a few loaves of bread and some fish. At that point, the disciples came to the conclusion that, although Jesus had good intentions, the food available was barely enough to feed Jesus and the 12 disciples, let alone thousands of people with empty stomachs.

William Wilberforce changed the world. Take a look at the story of this unlikely hero and the film documenting his life at *www.amazinggracemovie.com.*

The church seems to respond this way many times when problems are larger than our capacity to fix them. We say, "My $20 donation can't possibly make a difference!" or "What impact am I really having if I spend five hours a week serving special needs kids?" And we're right. Our possessions, time, and energy given in our strength cannot make a dent in the mountainous problems that plague our world. But any offering, no matter how small in the material world, can be multiplied exponentially in the hands of Jesus.

> Read Mark 12:41-44.
> Which offering was of more value?
>
> What does this tell us about the size of our offerings to God?

Jesus took the small offering of minimal food and made it overflow to abundant provision. Then He did something almost as surprising as the miracle itself. Rather than feeding the hungry with the newly multiplied loaves and fish Himself, Jesus placed the miraculous bounty into the hands of His followers. This is huge—Jesus could have easily sent manna down from heaven for all to eat as God did with the Israelites in the desert. He could have called all the people to Himself and fed them from His own hands. But instead, He gave the provision to His followers and instructed *them* to dispense the food to the people.

The provision was bountiful: "Everyone ate and was filled. Then they picked up 12 baskets full of leftover pieces! Now those who ate were about 5,000 men, besides women and children" (Matthew 14:20-21). What a beautiful picture of what Jesus wants to do with His church today. Jesus wants to provide in abundant fashion His gifts of hope, love, grace, sustenance, mercy, and justice, and He wants us to carry it to those in need. God both provides whatever is needed and empowers His people to do His will.

> Read 2 Corinthians 9:8.
> How much does God provide? For what good works?

Think for a moment what would have happened if the disciples had been handed baskets full of bread and fish and chose to sit down and gorge themselves on the massive buffet. "Thank you, Jesus!" they would say. "Thank you so much! You really shouldn't have . . . This is more than we can possibly eat. We are overwhelmed by your generosity!" Some of them might have even become a little territorial, slapping the hands of anyone trying to reach into "their" stash. Perhaps one disciple, through mouthfuls of food, would finally think to himself: *Jesus has really taken care of us to the point that we're not going to be able to finish all of this. I wonder what He's going to do about all these other people sitting around us who are still hungry? Isn't he going to help them too?*

Many of us in the U.S. are like the disciples I've just described in this imaginary scenario. We are awash in material, relational, and spiritual blessings. But instead of pouring out on others as Christ has called us to do we pray, "Thank You, thank You, thank You! Oh, that was much more than I expected! My life is awesome! I must be very special to you God." Then we casually ask, "God, why aren't you providing for other people around the world who are in great need? Don't you care about them?"

We, the children of God, are God's plan for pouring out His miracles on the needy and suffering in this world. God is not raining down manna from Heaven; He doesn't need to. His children have received the miracles of life, hope, and health. We just need to stop reveling in our abundance and begin to be the bearers of God's blessings.

How would you feel if you had been one of the disciples that day?

What would you have said to the people as you passed out the food?

God calls us to do great things in the world, but He does not do so out of need. He could feed all by Himself, but He's called us to be the conduit for the food. He could provide clothing and medicine by Himself, but He has given us the charge to take provision to those in need. In those terms, God's directive to us is not a burden; it's a blessing. He blesses us by pouring out through us. He fills us to overflowing.

## GO . . . AND GIVE

The people who are not experiencing the overflowing power of God are the ones that are holding tightly to what they have. Those who are experiencing the abundant life that God promises are the ones that are freely pouring out blessings on people who have need. Those blessings can be money, but just as important is the outpouring of conversation, time, prayer, energy, possessions, and materials. It doesn't matter what it is—if you have it, give it!

Right now you may be wondering, "How do I know if I'm doing too much or not enough?" That's a big question, right? The way you know if you're doing too much is simple: continuous prayer. There is simply no substitute for ongoing discussion with God.

As you consider God's plan for your life in relation to poverty, injustice, suffering, and hopelessness in the world, remember a these things:

1. The primary purpose for doing good works is to give credibility to the greatest message of all time—the gospel of Jesus Christ.

2. Learn to pray for God's direction in your activity, remembering that God will empower you to do the things He's called you to do.

3. Learn to say "yes" . . . and "no."

4. Don't do more (or less) than God has invited you to do.

5. Don't just listen to the Word and so deceive yourself; *do* what it says!

I close with the priestly blessing that God gave to Moses to tell Aaron and his sons: "The LORD bless you and protect you; the Lord make His face shine on you, and be gracious to you; the Lord look with favor on you and give you peace" (Numbers 6:24-26).

Remember, God will go with you as you do His work. Take hold of this opportunity to partner with Him and all the other saints to change the world through Christ.

# USE THIS JOURNAL AS A TOOL TO HELP YOU UNPACK THE MINISTRY OPPORTUNITY YOU'VE RECENTLY EXPERIENCED.

What I want to **tell** others about what I experienced is ...

Download Tim Hughes' song, **"God of Justice"** from the *Get Uncomfortable* playlist. The lyrics "Stepping forward / keep us from just singing / move us into action / We must go" are a call to action. What is your response to these lyrics? Why must you respond to injustice?

What **separates** you from impoverished individuals? Consider this passage: "The rich and the poor have this in common: the LORD made them both" (Proverbs 22:2).

Grab a copy of a news magazine or national newspaper. Clip articles and statements about poverty. Create a collage of statements and images that **represent poverty.** Add your own pictures.

**HOW WILL YOU PRAY DIFFERENTLY?**

"He raises the poor from the dust and lifts the needy from the garbage pile. He seats them with noblemen and gives them a throne of honor. For the foundations of the earth are the LORD's; He has set the world on them" (1 Samuel 2:8).

**I WISH I COULD SHAKE THE FEELING THAT . . .**

7
025

# CHOOSE A COLOR THAT YOU BELIEVE REPRESENTS POVERTY.

**CHOOSE A SHAPE** that you think represents people's perspective on poverty. Draw that shape and explain your choice.

Listen to the audio file **"OUR PLACE AT THE TABLE"**
from Session 1 again. How has your perspective
changed since you began this study?

"THE SPIRIT OF THE LORD GOD IS ON ME, BECAUSE THE LORD HAS ANOINTED ME TO BRING GOOD NEWS TO THE POOR. HE HAS SENT ME TO HEAL THE BROKENHEARTED, TO PROCLAIM LIBERTY TO THE CAPTIVES, AND FREEDOM TO THE PRISONERS" (ISAIAH 61:1).

7
025

Fredrich Buechner said,

## "GOD CALLS YOU TO A PLACE WHERE YOUR DEEP GLADNESS AND THE WORLD'S DEEP HUNGER MEET."

Describe how service to the least of

these contributes to your gladness.

Describe in detail the **PHYSICAL SURROUNDINGS** you found yourself in today. Use pictures if you'd like.

What **INCONVENIENCES** did you experience as you were preparing for your service project? During? Talk about it with someone in your study group.

Do you think your response to poverty will affect eternity? Proverbs 19:7 says, "Kindness to the poor is a loan to the LORD, and He will give a reward to the lender."

**THESE ARE A FEW OF MY HOPES:** Make a difference. Change a person's circumstance. Be Jesus. Talk less, do more. Educate. Eradicate. Be contagious. Live purposefully. Embrace the poor. See people, not their circumstance. Learn from the poor. Give more. Take less. Make a difference. Finish this list . . .

"OVERCOMING POVERTY IS NOT A GESTURE OF CHARITY. IT IS AN ACT OF JUSTICE. IT IS THE PROTECTION OF A FUNDAMENTAL HUMAN RIGHT, THE RIGHT TO DIGNITY AND A DECENT LIFE. WHILE POVERTY PERSISTS, THERE IS NO TRUE FREEDOM." — NELSON MANDELA

Check out the "Make Poverty History" Campaign online at
http://news.bbc.co.uk/1/hi/uk_politics/4232603.stm

# GROUP CONTACT INFORMATION

Name _____ Number _____
Email _____

Name _____ Number _____
Email _____

Name _____ Number _____
Email _____

Name _____ Number _____
Email _____

Name _____ Number _____
Email _____

Name _____ Number _____
Email _____

Name _____ Number _____
Email _____

Name _____ Number _____
Email _____

Name _____ Number _____
Email _____

Name _____ Number _____
Email _____

Name _____ Number _____
Email _____

Name _____ Number _____
Email _____

Name _____ Number _____
Email _____

Name _____ Number _____
Email _____

Name _____ Number _____
Email _____

Name _____ Number _____
Email _____

Name _____ Number _____
Email _____

Name _____ Number _____
Email _____

Name _____ Number _____
Email _____

Name _____ Number _____
Email _____

## END NOTES

1 Reggie McNeal, *Present Future* (San Francisco: Jossey-Bass, 2003), 32.

2 David D. Hall, Sydney E. Ahlstrom, *A Religious History of the American People*, 2004.

3 Gary Haugen, *Good News About Injustice* (Westmont: Intervarsity Press, 1999), 71.

4 Ibid. p. 72

5 Warren W. Wiersbe, *The Bible Exposition Commentary*
(Wheaton, : Victor Books, 1996), S. Lk 10:25.

6 Gary Haugen, *Good News About Injustice* (Westmont: Intervarsity Press, 1999), 95.

7 Matthew Henry, *Matthew Henry's Commentary on the Whole Bible :
Complete and Unabridged in One Volume* (Peabody: Hendrickson Publishers, 1996), S. 2 Co 5:16.

# What is Threads?

## WE ARE A COMMUNITY OF PEOPLE WHO ARE PIECING THE CHRISTIAN LIFE TOGETHER, ONE EXPERIENCE AT A TIME.

We're rooted in Romans 12 and Colossians 3. We're serious about worshipping God with our lives. We want to understand the grace Jesus extended to us on the cross and act on it. We want community, need to worship, and aren't willing to sit on our hands when the world needs help. We want to grow. We crave Bible study that raises questions, makes us think, and causes us to own our faith. We're interested in friendships that are as strong as family ties—the kind of relationships that transform individuals into communities.

Our Bible studies are designed specifically for you, featuring flexible formats with engaging video, audio, and music. These discussion-driven studies intentionally foster group and individual connections and encourage practical application of Scripture. You'll find topical articles, staff and author blogs, podcasts, and lots of other great resources at:

## THREADSMEDIA.COM

## STOP BY TO JOIN OUR ONLINE COMMUNITY— AND COME BY TO VISIT OFTEN!

### THE TOUGH SAYINGS OF JESUS
#### by Michael Kelley

This study explores four statements Jesus made that are difficult to grasp. Delving into the historical and cultural contexts of these Scriptures, the study focuses on sparking discussion and providing fresh insight, not pat answers. It will encourage you to embrace your doubts, and process through them, so that your faith can become deeper and stronger.

*Michael Kelley is a writer and traveling communicator who speaks to students and young adults throughout the United States. Passionate about effectively communicating the fullness of the good news of Jesus, Michael previously served as the principle teacher for Refuge, a weekly worship event for young adults in Nashville, Tennessee. Visit him at www.michaelkelleyonline.com.*

### IN TRANSIT
### WHAT DO YOU DO WITH YOUR WAIT?
#### by Mike Harder

Do you often feel that you're waiting for real life to begin? This study introduces you to three truths about waiting as it traces the lives of David, Jesus, and Joseph—all promised great things and all of whom waited, sometimes painfully, to see God's promises come to pass. You'll discover that waiting without purpose can lead to loneliness and doubting God, but purposeful waiting brings a sense of fulfillment and an awareness of God's timing and faithfulness.

*Mike Harder is a regular face and speaker at The Loop in Memphis, Tennessee, a weekly Bible study for young adults. He also serves on the staff of Highpoint Church overseeing the church's connection ministry. Find him at www.mikeharderministries.com.*

### THE EXCHANGE:
### TIRED OF LIVING THE CHRISTIAN LIFE ON YOUR OWN?
#### by Joel Engle

And exploration of Romans 6, 7, and 8, this study helps you understand that the power of the Christian life is found not in yourself or religious activity, but in "exchanging" your life for the life of Jesus Christ. You'll learn how to overcome sin and personal hang-ups through a life of dependency on Christ.

*Joel Engle is a worship communicator who uses his gifts to impact lives and glorify God. In The Exchange, Joel shares his own story of finally understanding what the Christian life is all about and learning to depend solely on Christ.*

For full details on all of Threads' studies, visit www.threadsmedia.com.

take a sneak peak at another study from Threads.

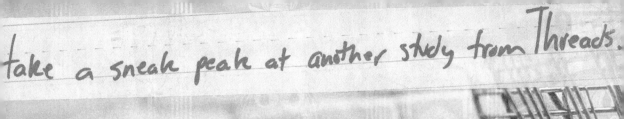

# EXCHANGE
## THE

### TIRED OF LIVING THE CHRISTIAN LIFE ON YOUR OWN?

*Joel Engle*

# EXCHANGE
## THE
### TIRED OF LIVING THE CHRISTIAN LIFE ON YOUR OWN?

## Entering the Exchange

### THE APPLE TREES

IMAGINE YOU ARE WALKING THROUGH AN APPLE ORCHARD IN EARLY SPRING. THE DELICATE FRAGRANCE OF THE APPLE BLOSSOM PERFUMES THE COOL MORNING AIR. THAT FLORAL SCENT IS ENOUGH TO TRIGGER MEMORY; YOU CLEARLY RECALL THE SWEET JUICY CHOMP OF THE RED DELICIOUS.

SUDDENLY, YOU STOP. IN THE HEIGHTENED SENSORY MOMENT, YOUR EARS GROW VERY SENSITIVE. THEY PROBE FOR ANY SOUND. WHAT DO YOU HEAR? NOTHING. TOTAL SILENCE.

AN APPLE (OR ANY KIND OF FRUIT) TREE IS ONE OF THE MOST MARVELOUS MYSTERIES IN THE WORLD. NO ONE CAN QUITE FATHOM THE EXQUISITE PERFECTION OF PHOTOSYNTHESIS; SOIL, SUNLIGHT, WATER, AND TEMPERATURES FLOW TOGETHER INTO A WONDROUS HARMONY OF CREATION. THE RESULT OF THIS SPLENDID FUSION IS THAT THE BLOSSOMS ON THE TREE SLOWLY MORPH INTO APPLES.

Incredibly, despite the great industry going on in those trees, they do it all effortlessly and silently. They don't work at it or have any form of apple anxiety. It is simply their nature to produce apples.

Apples happen naturally. Now, imagine another apple orchard. As you walk into it, you hear a low mumbling hum. At first, you wonder if insects are swarming the orchard. But as you stop near a particular apple tree, you hear a very distinct grunting. What? You move your head close to the branches. The grunting sound is coming from the tree itself! Yes, the apple tree is panting, then bearing down, and finally emitting a long agonizing growl.

You see, these are "Christian" apple trees. They've been taught that bearing apples is almost impossible, requires great straining, and is a "skill" which can easily be lost.

## THE LIE

Christian culture (especially in America) has created an outrageous, dangerous, and deadly lie about what life with Jesus is like. That lie goes something like this: our Father God is an elderly, somewhat senile, and angry Presence who lives in the swirling dark storm clouds.

True to His gloomy nature, He devised a sad, loveless, cruel and frankly impossible life for the "earthlings." He gave very specific and demanding rules for how to live that life. But He knew they would fail. He prepared a very hot and sulfuric lake of fire called "hell" for all those who (so naturally and inevitably) fail.

The lie goes on to explain what many call the "good news." The "good news," according to the lie, is that God finally realized that He must do something to give a legal way of escape from this very heavy and unhappy way of life. So His solution (which theologians try to explain, but we still don't quite understand) was to direct His Son Jesus to die for the sins of the people. As the obedient Son, Jesus did die; He paid the cost for our sin so that the people might—*might*—be saved.

So He died. The result of that death, at least in this cultural lie, is that humans can squeak into heaven by the skin of their teeth, if they can work hard enough to live up to Jesus' sacrifice. See, in this lie, even though Jesus died to deliver *new* life, *new* rules, and the *new* era of the Kingdom, the same harshness of the *old* still prevails. Despite the "New Testament" freshness, that lie still insists on an earthbound, grueling, human-centered scheme. That story ignores or denies the power of the superior life—that Jesus came to help the humans and has the power to do so. In the lie, Father God still required the very best and very strenuous efforts of people. He was still very severe and demanding.

The only difference is that, now, the people had to deal with the Son. If they didn't remember and keep all the new covenant rules and didn't try hard enough to be holy—through prayer and fasting, reading the Bible, and going to church a lot—they were still going to fall into that fiery furnace when they died.

## THE EXCHANGE

Perhaps you, too, have some misconceptions about Christianity that come from your culture rather than your Bible. So what is the truth?

Just as apple trees don't try to "have an apple," those who follow Christ aren't meant to will themselves to "live a Christian life." The main reason? No one can do it. Yes, you read that correctly. No one can live the Christian life.

One of the best kept secrets of the true Christian life is that Jesus actually lives His life through us; He does it all. He is the fullness of life and that superior life surges through our heart, our relationships, our attitudes, and our behaviors. That higher quality of life makes all things new. He doesn't just require something; He also provides what He requires.

Now, *that* is good news! Yes, of course, when He died He fulfilled the eternal requirements of a just God. But, in so doing, He took our life and nature onto Himself, nailed it to that tree, and then poured out His life so that we could all share it. Everyone who hears and responds is invited to cash in their life for His. The cross was the scene of a life exchange.

So there it is. That is the exchange. It's the essence of classical Christian faith. Yet, it has become covered over by the rubble of several centuries of Christian culture. I think three chapters of the Bible—Romans 6, 7, and 8—capture the simple, but transforming, reality of the Christian life better than anything else ever written. The Apostle Paul knocked the theological ball out of the park and on out of the earth's atmosphere.

Those Scriptures are a waterfall of revelation; they cascade in a thunderous roar from Heaven to earth. But so few people have ever heard these truths, much less embraced them as the right way to live. So strap yourself in. I want to pass on what the Lord has used to radically reorder my entire life. It was resurrection power to me. I know it can be to you also.

## TRUTH YOU CAN TRUST

A very wise man once said that truth which has not been lived in is stolen truth. In other words, if truth has not been broiled in the furnace of your own challenges and adversities, it will not nourish or sustain anyone else. You always know when you hear truth that was lived in; it carries that unmistakable ping of reality. It has become truth you can trust.

I know the exchange is true because it has been lived in my own life. I'll give you the details later, but I grew up so lonely, fearful, and unhappy that I was a seriously damaged kid. At 11 years old, I had no one to care for me. As an angry loner, I quickly decided that it all depended on me. Loneliness and anxiety can be so overwhelming that they suck all of life into a dark, bottomless, swirling void.

What I'm writing is not some cool theory. The truth in this book has been broiled, fried, and electrified in the laboratory of my own life. When I found the faith to just "give up" to God, I found that the kind and generous Savior was ready to move into my life and live through me. He made me a deal I couldn't refuse: "Give Me your life, and I'll give you Mine." Now my story is His story. He exchanged life with me.

In the exchange, you'll find a way of life which flows out as naturally as apples stream from the branches of the tree. The result is a continuing harvest of sweetness, flavor, and full-throttle joy.

**The Exchange**

## HOW TO READ THIS BOOK

Finally, I want to explain the idea of this book and give some suggestions on how to read it. I wholeheartedly believe the truth of the apple tree. That tree is part of a larger inter-related dynamic of creation. There is nothing tentative or fragile about that synergistic process. As I've explained, all of that happens naturally and effortlessly. Apples appear because of the inherent nature of the tree as part of that living cycle.

That is the precise principle that Jesus taught when He wrote that He is the true vine and His disciples are the branches. The surging power of life is in Him, and that power flows out through all those who are the branches of the Vine. That is Jesus' explanation of the exchange (you'll find it in John 15).

Either you accept the principle of the apple tree or you don't, but everything past this point in the book builds from that orchard. If you do accept this truth, then what is written in the pages of this book can bring you closer to maturity in your walk with Christ.

Also, my writing style is probably somewhat like that of a basketball coach. Like a coach, I am primarily concerned with equipping you to reach your full potential. I see it as my job to drive and help you on your way to maturity as followers of Christ. Further, I won't treat you like infants; I am direct and use words like *should* and *must* and *stop* and *no*. I tell you that you may "have to" do some things. I want you to grow up.

Know also that this book is meant to be read, put down, and then read again. There are so many profound thoughts throughout Romans 6, 7 and 8 that you may want to take some time and marinate in them for a while. You can read it in large chunks like any other book, but it is also designed to be read as quick cuts—maybe as you ride the bus, wait in line at the airport, wait for your friends at Starbucks, or sit in the beauty or barber chair. You see, I'm a musician; I tend to think of CD or MP3 "cuts." You can listen to the whole CD or you can listen to one cut at a time as you wait in the drive-up lane at the bank.

Finally, this is a "living" book. New chapters are being written by you in the rhythm of your own life. You will touch and experience dimensions of the exchange that I have never considered.

Please tell me your stories. I'm serious; I want to know how you touch the exchange, what it means to you, how it changes your world and makes all things new. I'm interested in your setbacks as well as your successes. You can email me at *joel@joelengle.com*.

May God bless you and open your heart and mind as you step into the waters of *The Exchange*.